VITAL DOCTRINES
OF
THE FAITH

by
MALCOLM FURNESS

William B. Eerdmans Publishing Company
Grand Rapids, Michigan

Preface

This little book is intended to provide a convenient summary of the origin, development and significance of the principal doctrines of the Faith, which will be of use both to the non-technical reader who wants to know something of the processes through which theology has evolved, and to those beginning the serious study of Dogmatics, who want a short and straightforward introduction to the subject. If the volume serves to stimulate the ordinary churchman's interest in biblical and historical theology, and to encourage a wider and deeper study of those doctrines which represent the Christian view of God and man, and the world in which men live, it will have done all it set out to do.

Acknowledgement is due to my friends, Dr. P. G. E. Bell and the Reverend Arthur Bott, for valuable comments on sections of the typescript, and to my former tutors, Dr. N. H. Snaith and Principal A. R. George, who read the whole manuscript and generously gave me the benefit of their wisdom and scholarship. To them, to the ancient and modern theologians on whom every student draws, and to Dr. Cecil Northcott of the Lutterworth Press, who first suggested that this book should be written, and who has since given encouragement at every stage, I gratefully own a considerable debt. For the errors and shortcomings that may remain, the author alone is responsible.

J.M.F.

Gosforth,
Newcastle upon Tyne,
Whitsuntide, 1972.

Abbreviations

ET	English Text.
Gk.	Greek.
apoc.	apocalyptic.
Apoc.	Apocalypse.
Heb.	Hebrew.
LXX.	The Septuagint Version.
NEB	The New English Bible.
NT	The New Testament.
OT	The Old Testament.
RC	Roman Catholic.
Shab.	Shabbath—Sabbath.
Taan.	Taanith—Fast.

PART ONE

THE DOCTRINE OF GOD

I

GOD THE FATHER

1. Biblical

Christian theology depends primarily upon God's self-revelation, and the best starting point in any discussion of the doctrine of God is probably the appearance in the burning bush in Exodus Chapter 3. There God's name is given as YHWH,[1] from the root meaning *to be*. Moses is to tell the Children of Israel "I AM has sent me". In other words, God is being, the source of being, the soul of reality,[2] but the Being is a *personal* being, and the Reality a saving reality, for the theophany at Horeb is not only a revelation of God's name but a declaration of His benevolent purpose.

"I have surely seen the affliction of my people . . . and I am come down to save them": this is the keynote of Scripture—Bible history is salvation history, the record of what God has done for man's redemption, and everything in nature and experience is seen in the light of Yahweh's gracious purpose. The heavens may declare the glory of God, but it is the glory of a God who pities His children, leads His flock like a shepherd and is constantly seeking to reclaim the lost. The wonder

[1] The *tetragrammaton*. The vowels (not written in ancient Hebrew) are uncertain, but the form *Yahweh* is often adopted as being more accurate than the familiar *Jehovah*.

[2] Cf. Acts 17:28.

7

of creation is not its complexity, but its *raison d'être*, that God made the world to be man's home. Accordingly, the doctrine of creation is not primary, and Hebrew emphasis is not upon such attributes as omnipotence and omniscience etc. which are philosophically appropriate to a Prime Mover or Great Designer, but on the personal and moral qualities associated with redemptive love and with a Being who can be called Husband, Father and Friend.

The twin concepts of personality and saving love are basic to the Hebrew doctrine of God the Father which, in turn, is the foundation of New Testament theology. Yahweh is often enough depicted in anthropomorphic terms—He has a mighty arm, His nose burns with anger, but this is not because the Israelites thought of God as man writ large; rather it is an attempt to express the intensely personal nature of One who is no aloof, unfeeling deity, but a Redeemer-God who enters into active and intimate relationships with men, who will look for Adam in the garden, call Abraham His friend and talk with Moses face to face. That is not to say that Yahweh is wholly immanent: indeed, He is a transcendent Being, majestic and awe-inspiring; but transcendence does not make Him remote. He is the One who inhabits eternity, but who also dwells with those of a humble and contrite spirit.[1] From the outset, God is revealed as the sort of deity who might well, in the fulness of time, become incarnate and dwell among us.

The Holiness of God. God's transcendence is expressed in terms of holiness, the root meaning of which is *separate*. God is not man, His thoughts are not our thoughts, nor His ways our ways,[2] and the difference between God and man is not simply one of scale, but of radical "otherness": there is none like unto Yahweh. This transcendent other-ness is, moreover, primarily moral. Yahweh is of eyes too pure to behold iniquity;[3] righteousness is the mainspring of His being and

[1] Isa. 57:15.   [2] Isa. 55:8f.   [3] Hab. 1:13.

finds expression in a constancy of loving-kindness[1] which (rather than any inert neutrality) is what the Bible means by His unchangeableness. What theologians sometimes call the "relative attributes"[2] of God—omnipotence, omniscience, omnipresence etc.—can undoubtedly be found in Scripture, for His power, knowledge and presence are not subject to any externally imposed limitation; but they are not central to what the Prophets and Psalmists had to say about God. The thing that matters is that Yahweh is the Holy One of Israel, unchanging in His constancy of righteous love which wills the salvation of men; God is supremely Father, and to His fatherly purposes His power, knowledge and presence are ever bent.

God's Covenant Love. The constancy of God's love and the perfection of His holiness alike find expression in covenant. Divine love is no chancy affair, but is made to depend upon an agreement which He makes with man. The covenant of Horeb/Sinai[3] made with Moses is the classic example, but earlier covenants with Abram[4] and Noah[5] extend the scope to cover all mankind. God will be our God, and we are to be His people, but because Yahweh is holy, covenant demands obedience to His righteous law. The holiness that God requires of men is not, certainly, His moral perfection, much less His "Goddishness", but it is a degree of moral earnestness: to the Hebrew, religion without morality would have been almost a contradiction in terms. Morality is not the whole of religion, but it is a necessary part, and Israel is not allowed to forget that the loving-kindness of God is "to such as keep His covenant and remember His commandments to do them".

Creation and Providence. As already indicated, the doctrine of creation arose quite late in the development of Hebrew

[1] Ps. 36:5–10; Ps. 138 etc.
[2] i.e., the attributes that describe His relationship with the world.
[3] Ex. 34:28.   [4] Gen. 15:18.   [5] Gen. 9:9–17.

9

religion, and the creative act was understood in the light of what was already known of the nature of God, not *vice versa*. The older of the two accounts of creation[1] makes it clear that God's object was the creation of man: in other words, creation was but the first of a whole series of mighty acts in which His benevolent purpose appears, and must therefore be seen in relation to the whole benign activity of God which we call providence.

This providence is seen in two aspects. On the one hand, Yahweh sustains the world He has made, daily and yearly renewing the nature of man and beast, keeping the planets on their courses, making the Sun rise on the evil and the good, and generally providing for the birds of the heavens and the flowers of the field.[2] On the other hand, His spiritual provision for man is evidenced by the deliverance of Israel from Egypt, the mission of a succession of prophets, the reforming experience of the Exile[3] and, in the New Testament, by the Incarnation, death and Resurrection of God's Son. Throughout Hebrew religious history, God has been engaged in a saving dialogue with man exquisitely summarized in Jesus's parable of the *Wicked Husbandmen*.[4]

The New Testament confirms the Hebrew doctrine of a loving Father-God only this time, in the face of Jesus Christ, we see more clearly than ever before what God is like: He is like Jesus, who is "the express image of His person".[5] The God of the New Testament still seeks man's salvation and requires man's moral response, but now we see the Father's purpose as one that will not stop short of the ultimate sacrifice, and His moral requirement as one that man must satisfy not by his own unaided effort, but by the grace of Christ. The last word is with the Fourth Evangelist:

[1] Gen. 2:4ff.
[2] Job 38; Ps. 104; Isa. 40:12, 22, 26; Mt. 5:45; 6:26, 30.
[3] The Exile in Babylon, 586–536 BC.
[4] Mk. 12:1ff.   [5] Heb. 1:3.

For God so loved the world, that he gave his only begotten Son, that whosoever believeth in him should not perish, but have eternal life. (Jn. 3:16)

2. Historical Development

The Early Church was largely pre-occupied with Christology —the relationship of the Incarnate Son to the Eternal Father and to the whole economy of the Holy Trinity, and except in these ways, little was added to the understanding of the nature of God. As theology became more philosophical (in its attempts to synthesize Hebraic and Greek thought), churchmen began to speculate about the relative attributes of God, and especially about the conflict between Divine immutability and the changes involved in God's breaking into time by the act of Incarnation. From time to time[1] there was an attempt to assert *Divine impassibility* (the doctrine that God cannot suffer), though this was exceedingly difficult to reconcile with biblical texts that spoke of His pity or anger, and made very real difficulties for the doctrine of the Atonement. Despite misgivings about Divine changelessness, however, the Fatherhood of God and His loving purpose in creation and redemption were never really in question.

At least, the doctrine was not seriously in question until discoveries in astronomy (Copernicus, Tycho Brahe, Kepler, Galileo) and the advance of natural science (Bacon and Newton), themselves the result of the Renaissance of learning and the later intellectual awakening of the eighteenth-century Enlightenment, brought Faith and Reason into sharp conflict. In England the conflict gave rise to Deism, a system that accepted the existence of God but stressed *natural religion* as against *revealed* truth.[2] On the Continent, it led to a wider

[1] E.g., Ignatius (*c.* A.D. 112) and Clement of Alexandria (*c.* A.D. 200).
[2] E.g., Toland, *Christianity not Mysterious* (1696); Tindal, *Christianity as old as the Creation* (1730).

11

movement that left rationalism supreme (in the Protestant churches, at least) until, at the beginning of the nineteenth century, Schleiermacher's[1] emphasis on Faith redressed the balance. In the nineteenth century, Lyell's work in geology[2] and Darwin's on biological evolution[3] brought the biblical doctrine of creation into doubt and led to a conflict between science and religion that was only gradually resolved as men became more aware that biblical doctrine is concerned not to give a scientific account of the origin of the universe, but to explain its existence in terms of the *purpose*, not the method, of the Creator.

While science can challenge theism by denying the *need* of a God to account for the existence of the universe (though, indeed, natural phenomena hardly constitute a *universe* without some unifying purpose!), and while, especially in the last century, many became agnostics or atheists on scientific grounds, science can say nothing about the *nature* of any God there may be. Philosophy, on the other hand, has had a great deal to say about God. In Patristic and Medieval times, Platonism and Aristotelianism radically influenced Christian thought, and in more modern times, existentialism[4] and logical positivism[5] have had their effect, culminating in the most recent "Death of God" theology.[6] The latter, extremely vulnerable on philosophical and logical grounds, is so radical

[1] F. Schleiermacher, *Reden, Addresses on Religion to its Cultured Despisers* (1799).

[2] *Principles of Geology* (1830–33).

[3] *Origin of Species* (1859).

[4] Especially since Kierkegaard (1813–1855).

[5] E.g., A. J. Ayer, *Language, Truth and Logic*, 2nd Edn. (1946). For a pungent criticism of logical positivism and linguistic philosophy in general, see E. Gellner, *Words and Things* (1959).

[6] Leading works of this School include D. Bonhoeffer, *Letters and Papers from Prison* (1959); W. Hamilton, *The New Essence of Christianity*; T. J. J. Altizer, *Gospel of Christian Atheism*; P. van Buren, *The Secular Meaning of the Gospel* (1963).

12

as to be quite outside the scope of any discussion of mainstream theology.

3. Constructive Statement

Theology must, by definition, have a God to study, and it is no accident that all the great world religions begin with a *given*, a revelation contained in their authoritative scriptures: that is the justification for beginning where we began, with a biblical text. This is the only way to proceed if we are to arrive at belief in the sort of God who can fitly be the object of devotion. Reason may lead us to believe that the universe and the world of men are more plausibly explained by reference to the will of a purposeful Being than as the more or less arbitrary result of random processes of cause and effect. Philosophy can tell us *a priori* that *if* there is a God responsible for natural phenomena, then that God must have certain attributes of power, knowledge, presence and so on, but at best this rational approach will lead to Deism, belief in a God who made the universe much as a man might make a watch. The righteous, holy God of Christian theology must remain the object of faith.

Faith and Reason. That is not to say that belief in such a God is irrational, but that it is para-rational. The traditional "proofs" of the existence of God based on design, the universality of moral sanctions and the necessary existence of the most perfect Being,[1] undoubtedly have strong cumulative force, but they are evidences, not proofs. Ultimate values such as truth and beauty are in principle unprovable, and as the artist must be content to *believe* in the reality of beauty and meaning, the philosopher in the existence of truth, and the scientist in the strictly invariable operation of cause and effect, none of which is susceptible of logical demonstration,

[1] Respectively, the *teleological*, *moral* and *ontological* arguments.

so the theologian must be prepared to accept the existence of God and to build his system upon what scripture and experience tell him. Religious truth is *revealed* truth.

Having once embarked upon a voyage of faith in which the point of departure is the biblical revelation of God, however, the theologian must bring reason to bear upon both revelation and experience. The data of faith are *given*; what do they mean? That is theology's task, and to that task the scholar must bring all his mental powers if, upon the foundation of faith, he is to build a coherent and satisfying theological explanation of the world and of life as he knows it. Only when he loves the God of revelation with all his mind as well as with all his heart and soul will he begin to make sense of life and arrive at a Faith that he can both assert and defend without doing violence to the rational powers with which that God has endowed him. To put the matter another way, the Christian thinker begins with the Redeemer-God of biblical revelation and, guided always by scripture and experience, slowly and reverently thinks his way to a world-view, based on Faith and informed by Reason, in which all the tenets of the Faith that we shall have to consider can find a proper place.

2

GOD THE SON (INCARNATION)

The doctrine of the *Incarnation*[1] is the belief that Jesus of Galilee was the Son of God in human form, and the branch of theology that studies Christ's divine/human nature is called *Christology*. Christian teaching that Jesus is both human and divine, both the Man from Nazareth and the Second Person of the Trinity, is the result of theological reflection upon the experience of the first disciples, who began by regarding Jesus as Teacher and Leader and went on to worship Him as God. At Caesarea Philippi, Peter spoke for the others when he said of Jesus "Thou art the Christ, the Son of the living God",[2] a sentiment that was echoed by Thomas, after the Resurrection, in the confession "My Lord and my God".[3] Respect and reverence had given way to adoration as they had come to know more fully who He was.

In line with this discovery, the Early Church required its members to affirm that "Jesus is Lord" (*Kürios Christos*), deliberately choosing the title that the Septuagint[4] used of

[1] Latin *in–carnē* (flesh).
[2] Mt. 16:16.
[3] Jn. 20:28.
[4] The Septuagint (LXX), or Version of the Seventy, a Greek translation of the OT made, probably, before 150 B.C.

15

Yahweh, and the Roman world gave to the saviour-gods of the pagan mystery religions, but it is a far cry from this simple creed to the careful statement of the Definition of Chalcedon (A.D. 451) which became the standard of Christological orthodoxy:

> ... One and the same Son, our Lord Jesus Christ, at once complete in Godhead and complete in manhood, truly God and truly man, consisting also of a reasonable soul and body; of one substance with the Father as regards his Godhead, and at the same time of one substance with us as regards his manhood; like us in all respects, apart from sin; as regards his Godhead, begotten of the Father before the ages, but yet as regards his manhood ... begotten ... of Mary the Virgin, the God-bearer; one and the same Christ, Son, Lord, Only-begotten, recognised in two natures, without confusion, without change, without division, without separation; the distinction of natures being in no way annulled by the union, but rather the characteristics of each nature being preserved and coming together to form one person and substance, not as parted or separated into two persons, but one and the same son and Only-begotten God the Word, Lord Jesus Christ.

Between the time when Paul wrote the first Christian documents and the close of the Council of Chalcedon, Christology had been hammered out, but the formulae of Church Councils were not strict deductions from the words of the New Testament; they were the result of long and sometimes acrimonious theological debate, and were expressed not in the language of Scripture, but in the thought-forms of the prevailing Hellenistic philosophy.

1. Biblical

The New Testament foreshadows later Catholic doctrine. Paul can say ... *God was in Christ reconciling the world unto himself* (2 Cor. 5:19) and ... *in him* (Christ) *dwelleth all the*

16

fulness of the Godhead bodily (Col. 2:9). He can speak of ...
*the light of the knowledge of the glory of God in the face of Jesus
Christ* (2 Cor. 4:6) while fuller statements are found in the
prologues to the Fourth Gospel and to Hebrews:

> In the beginning was the Word (*Logos*), and the Word was with
> God, and the word was God ... All things were made through
> him ... And the Word became flesh and dwelt among us (and we
> beheld his glory, glory as of the only begotten from the Father),
> full of grace and truth. (Jn. 1:1, 3, 14)

> ... His Son, whom he appointed heir of all things, through whom
> also he made the worlds; who being the effulgence of his glory,
> and the very image of his substance, and upholding all things by
> the word of his power ... (Heb. 1:2f.)

Here are the bare bones of Christology, but they do not add
up to a formed doctrine of the Person of Jesus Christ, at once
human and divine; or rather, they endorse the doctrine without explaining exactly how the Galilean Carpenter came to
be the pre-existent Son of God, or how the divine and the
human cohered in His personality. The New Testament
writers were content to call Jesus "Son of God" (Mark) or
"Emmanuel" ("God with us")[1] and even where, as in John
and Hebrews, something more was attempted, there was no
thought of laying down a hard and fast doctrine of Christ's
Person. The Jesus of Christian experience was the fulfilment
of Messianic hopes; He was the one who was to come; He
was both God and man. That was the fact to be proclaimed,
and they did not care to speculate about the *how* of it.

2. Historical Development

The First Five Centuries. Those who did care to speculate had
to do justice to both the divinity and the humanity of
Christ. Inevitably one or other was from time to time lost
sight of. Theoretically, the Church came to believe in a

[1] Matthew.

17

Christ who had two full natures combined in one undivided Person, but quite soon theologians settled into two main schools. Alexandrian scholars stressed the divinity of Christ at the expense of His humanity, while with theologians at Antioch it was the other way about, and practically all the Christological heresies that arose in the Early Church were extreme expressions of one view or the other. The main heresies of the Antiochene type were:

Arianism (condemned by the Council of Nicaea, A.D. 325), which denied the *eternal existence* of Christ, and therefore His full divinity. The arch-heretic was Arius and the champion of orthodoxy, Athanasius. Through Imperial support, Arianism at one time almost swept the church, and Athanasius seemed to stand alone.

Nestorianism (condemned by the Council of Ephesus, A.D. 431) denied the combination of the human and divine natures in the *one person* of Christ, and left Him as a God-bearing man. Nestorius was Bishop of Constantinople, and his orthodox opponent Cyril, Bishop of Alexandria.

Heresies of the opposite (Alexandrian) type were:

Docetism, an early error which asserted that Christ's body was unreal and His suffering and death therefore *only an appearance*. This heresy, which would have undermined the whole gospel, was vigorously condemned by Ignatius, Bishop of Antioch (*c.* A.D. 112). *Apollinarianism* (condemned by the Council of Constantinople, A.D. 381) held that Christ had *no human soul*, its place being supplied by the *Logos*, or active Word of God. This implied, of course, that Christ was not fully man. The heretic was Bishop of Laodicea, and his catholic opponent Basil, Bishop of Caesarea. *Eutychianism* (condemned at Chalcedon, A.D. 451), an extreme expression of Alexandrian Christology, which *denied the two natures* of Christ and in effect laid sole stress on the divine nature. This heresy is the opposite of Nestorianism. Eutyches was an elderly monk of Constantinople and his principal catholic opponent Leo, Bishop of Rome.

It was almost impossible for the early theologians to keep their balance on the tight-rope that stretched over the chasms of heresy, and their difficulty was at least partly that of vocabulary. Substance (Gk. *ousia*), nature (*phüsis*) and person (*hüpostasis*) were not ideal terms, and the incessant wrangling over them seems to us very artificial. A reverent agnosticism about the details of the divine psychology would have been less presumptuous and more seemly. A greater handicap was the Greek notion of the immutability of God that had become a firm tenet of theology: clearly, if God is strictly unchanging, a real incarnation is impossible! That was the root trouble. Scripture speaks of God as unchanging, but it is His *nature of love* that is constant, and there is no arbitrary restriction of His freedom of *action*. It was when the emphasis shifted from practical Hebraic concern with what God had *done* to Greek metaphysical speculation about what He might consistently do, that theology got into really deep water.

The Definition of Chalcedon was an ingenious compromise. Jesus Christ was "of one substance" (*homöousios*) with God in regard to His divine nature, and with us in respect of His human nature. The famous four adverbs, *without confusion*, *without change*, *without division*, *without separation*, were designed to guard against extreme Alexandrian theology on the one hand and the extreme Antiochene position on the other, but they were entirely negative, and the whole Definition did not constitute a coherent Christology, nor did it put an end to controversy. In allowing to the Virgin Mary the title *theotokos*—"mother of God", itself the subject of strong controversy, the Council demonstrated its own logical pedantry, and its remoteness from the simplicity of the New Testament. The logic is clear enough; if the divine and human natures of Christ were inseparable and Mary was the mother of the one, she must therefore be the mother of both. But however sound the conclusion, "mother of God" is hardly what Mary's cousin, Elisabeth, can have meant in Luke 1:43!

Chalcedon Onwards. Heresies continued to arise—*Monophysitism* (Christ had only *one nature*), and *Monothelitism* (only *one will*)—and to be condemned, and a Church weakened by theological strife crumbled before the advance of Islam. Nestorian and Monophysite churches continued to exist in the East, as they do to this day, only now they are accepted as orthodox.[1] In the eighth century, attempts at pacification were made by suggesting that the human nature of Christ found its personality in the *Logos* (*en hüpostasia*), or that in the union each nature shared its properties with the other (*communicatio idiomatum*)—the one theory very near to Apollinarianism, the other verging on Eutychianism!

The great Medieval theologian, Thomas Aquinas (A.D. 1225–1274), enslaved again by ideas of divine immutability, held Christological views which so stressed the divinity of Christ that they were at times almost docetic. Even in the Virgin's womb, Christ possessed omniscience! Admittedly, Medieval piety laid great stress upon the human suffering of Christ, and Anselm's theory of the Atonement required a Saviour who was truly man; but the Church did not really come to terms with God in the flesh. The grip of Greek ideas had tightened. Now it was not simply divine immutability that was the problem; philosophical distaste for the material and the physical,[2] made it even harder to accept a Christ who was flesh of our flesh.

The Reformation. Two main streams of Protestantism flow from the Reformation, the Lutheran and the Calvinist (or

[1] Some of these, now referred to as "non-Chalcedonian" churches, are members of the World Council of Churches.

[2] Partly responsible for the encouragement of celibacy and the growth of Monasticism.

Reformed) traditions. Broadly, Lutheranism took the Alexandrian position, stressing the divinity of our Lord, making great play with the idea of *communicatio idiomatum*, and therefore leaning in an Apollinarian direction. By interaction, the two natures functioned as one, and the dominant influence was certainly divine. Calvinism was much more Antiochene, and the two natures of Christ were kept so distinct that Lutheran critics sometimes said they were like two planks glued together! In Reformed Christology, the *Logos* was in Christ, but not all of the Logos: the Word of God was not *totally* incarnate, but had also a continuing separate existence. Calvinist emphasis was almost bound to be on the humanity of Christ.

Modern Kenotic Theories. Roman Catholicism is still largely under the spell of Thomist theology,[1] and Catholic emphasis on the Virgin Birth, the Immaculate Conception of Mary, and God offered up in the Mass, all point to the divinity rather than the humanity of Jesus Christ. Protestantism, on the other hand, has tended to stress the humanity of Christ: Unitarianism and the Jehovah Witness movement are extreme expressions of this view, and amount almost to modern Arianism.

A brave attempt to solve the problem is that of the *Kenotic* school, which bases its theory on two Pauline texts:

> Who, being in the form of God, counted it not a prize to be on an equality with God, But emptied himself, taking the form of a servant, being made in the likeness of men. (Phil. 2:6f.)

> Though he was rich, yet for your sakes he became poor, that ye through his poverty might became rich. (2 Cor. 8:9)

and also upon the whole gospel picture of a Christ who could be weary, hungry, surprised—who had to confess

[1] i.e. the theology of Thomas Aquinas. . . .

21

ignorance, and yet who was conscious of his divinity. Kenotic Christology[1] holds that Christ voluntarily emptied himself, at the Incarnation, of the relative attributes of omnipotence, omniscience and omnipresence while retaining the essential attributes of holiness and love. That, at least, was the view of the Lutheran, Thomasius, published in 1853. Gess, a Calvinist (1856), was more radical; laying aside *all* His attributes, the Logos *became* a human soul. In other words, Christ's cosmic functions were temporarily suspended; presumably they were assumed by the Father or the Holy Spirit. At the Incarnation, Christ suffered a total extinction of His divine consciousness, only regaining it after a course of time as a fitful human consciousness. A middle position was taken by Martensen, a Danish Lutheran (1856), who held that as a result of the kenosis Christ retained His Godhead in a limited fashion, but the Logos still continued to function cosmically— an oddly Calvinist view!

British kenoticists include A. M. Fairbairn (1893), Bishop Gore (1898), P. T. Forsyth (1909)[2] and H. R. Mackintosh (1912)[3], and in the writings of the last two the theory is presented in its most attractive form. Forsyth sees the divine attributes not as renounced at the Incarnation, but as retracted from the actual to the potential. In the Incarnate Christ, the attributes are concentrated, and the kenosis is accompanied by a plerosis, a process of gradual reintegration through which, by genuine moral effort, Christ regained the mode of being that He had voluntarily laid aside. Perhaps more than any earlier Christological writer, Forsyth makes sense of the spiritual struggles of Christ.

Mackintosh rejects Thomasius's distinction between *relative* and *essential* attributes, and like Forsyth, speaks of the divine

---

[1] The classical English account of kenotic theories is by A. B. Bruce, *The Humiliation of Christ* (5th edn., 1900).

[2] *The Person and Place of Jesus Christ.*

[3] *The Doctrine of the Person of Jesus Christ.*

qualities not as abandoned, but retained in potential rather than actual form; during the Incarnation they functioned in new ways. Only in mature manhood, and then fitfully, did the Incarnate Son know His divinity, "which must have remained for Him an object of *faith* to the very end".[1] Nothing is said about the Logos or the Son apart from the Incarnation because Scriptural evidence is insufficient. Anticipating the question, "What happened to the cosmic functions of the Logos while He was Incarnate, if Incarnation involved kenosis?" Mackintosh appeals to Augustine's principle, that outwardly the works of the Trinity are inseparable. To the objection of Ritschl, that in His earthly existence the kenoticist Christ had no Godhead at all, Mackintosh replies that the absence of certain qualities is necessary for *any* advent of God in time.

3. Constructive Statement

Trenchant criticism of kenotic Christology, especially by Archbishop Temple[2] and D. M. Baillie,[3] made the theory unfashionable for a time, but no convincing alternative was advanced, and more recently the theory has been vigorously defended by Vincent Taylor.[4] Probably, as J. M. Creed remarked, most people who have a Christology they would care to defend, are kenoticists at heart, and certainly, if we are to take the gospel record of Christ's earthly life seriously and at the same time believe that the figure who was so perfectly human was also truly divine, some form of kenosis is inevitable. Early Continental exponents of the theory erred in being too precise about what was involved in the act of kenosis, but the British scholars' unwillingness to speculate

[1] *Op. cit.*, 481.
[2] *Christus Veritas* (1924).
[3] *God was in Christ* (1948).
[4] *The Person of Christ in New Testament Teaching* (1958).

about which particular attributes were dispensable and which not, or to presume to delve into the divine psychology makes them much less vulnerable. Kenotic theory at least allows us to make sense of the earthly Christ's confessed limitations, to believe in an Incarnate Son who could be tempted and feel God-forsaken, and to do it on no other supposition than a divine condescension entirely consonant with what we know of God's nature of love. That the Fathers did not choose to base a kenotic theory on the two Pauline texts, is no objection; they were held back, as we have seen, by misplaced loyalty to prevailing philosophical ideas. However metaphysically attractive divine immutability may be, it is not a biblical doctrine. Nor is it a valid objection to protest, as Temple did, that kenoticism raises difficulties for the doctrine of the Holy Trinity. Trinitarian doctrine exists to explain the biblical data, not *vice versa*, and if kenotic Christology appears amenable to what the New Testament teaches about the Incarnation, then Trinitarian theology must come to terms with it.

Scripture and experience must be the arbiters of faith and doctrine in every generation, and Scripture must be the final court of appeal in which experience is tested. What we have seen of attempts to formulate a coherent and consistent Christology in the Early Church, at the Reformation and in modern times illustrates again and again the failure of attempts to define exactly what the Bible leaves undefined. As there is in the New Testament no definitive theory of the Atonement, so there is no precise theology of the Incarnation. What we have is a very firm insistence upon the true divinity and the real humanity of Christ. Scripture asserts and faith confirms that the Son of God took our flesh upon Him and dwelt among us, that in the earthly Christ dwelt all the fulness of the Godhead bodily—that is, all the fulness that His humanity could contain. That, no doubt, is as far as we can go with certainty and without presumption.

THE VIRGIN BIRTH[1]

The doctrine, contained in both the Creeds in the article—
... *conceived (Incarnate) by the Holy Ghost, born of the Virgin
Mary* ... rests on comparatively slender New Testament
evidence. The earliest writings (Paul's letters) and the first
Gospel (Mark's) are silent on the subject. Luke, a doctor, in
whom Mary may well have found it easier to confide,
mentions the circumstance in his Gospel,[2] but not in Acts, and
certainly no use was made of the story in the earliest
Christian preaching. This silence has led some scholars to
doubt the fact, while others maintain that since the Church
made no use of the doctrine when formulating its Christology,
there can have been no point in inventing the story. Nor is it
likely that the story was manufactured to suit the prophecy of
Isaiah 7:14, which speaks only of a "young woman" (*alma*),
not necessarily a maiden.

The theological value of the doctrine is doubtful. On the
one hand, there is a certain appropriateness in the idea that
Jesus Christ derived His divine nature from the Holy Spirit,
His human nature from a woman; on the other hand, it
can be argued that Jesus would be fully man only if He had
two human parents. The miraculous nature of the story is
itself no problem. The Incarnation is a unique event and
therefore we cannot say how it ought to take place: the birth
of the God/man might well involve unusual biological
processes! In any case, the Incarnation itself, however viewed,
is a tremendous miracle, and is made no more difficult by this
particular addition.

[1] This doctrine should not be confused with the RC dogma of the
Immaculate Conception, which refers to the circumstances of *Mary's*
birth. The dogma is, of course, rejected by Protestants.

[2] The only NT refs. are Lk. 1:34ff. and Mt. 1:18–25.

25

It is often objected that miraculous circumstances are related in connection with the birth of various classical heroes, but direct comparison shows at once that such stories are far removed from the restrained accounts of Luke and Matthew.[1] The credal statements are equally restrained, and were most likely intended to safeguard the real humanity of Jesus (and to exclude docetic notions), rather than to define the precise means by which the Incarnation was achieved.

The present writer accepts the doctrine, but since it was no part of the apostolic *kērūgma* (proclamation), it can hardly be regarded as vital doctrine. Christians must believe in the divinity of Jesus Christ and the reality of the Incarnation, but should be allowed to remain uncommitted about the method adopted by God.

---

[1] Pagan myths generally speak of children resulting from sexual intercourse between gods (or goddesses) and humans—hardly *virgin* birth! Such unions are invariably based on desire or lust. In classical mythology, Aeneas was the son of a man and a goddess, Heracles the child of a god and a woman. The kings of Egypt were similarly said to be sons of a god and a human mother.

3

THE HOLY SPIRIT

1. Biblical

The Old Testament. The Spirit of God is His power operative in the world, the aspect of divine activity turned towards man, and because the Spirit is inseparable from God, biblical understanding of His nature and function changes as the doctrine of God develops. The Hebrew word for spirit is *ruach*, literally, *breath* or *wind*, and in primitive Israelitish religion, God's Spirit was thought of in animistic fashion; the wind was Yahweh's breath, the storm an explosion of His wrath. It was always the unusual and striking that first attracted men's attention and awakened religious awe, and in early Hebrew religion the operation of God's Spirit in man was looked for in the para–normal and the abnormal—in the ecstasy of a prophet, the moods of the madman, as well as in exceptional physical strength, notable feats of skill and outstanding powers of leadership.[1]

Only gradually, as Yahweh came to be recognized as more than a tribal God and, moreover, as a God whose actions were not random or capricious but directed towards a steady redemptive purpose, did men come to see His Spirit as responsible for the creation and moral renewal of man. The

[1] Num. 24:2ff.; 1 Sam. 10:1–13; 11:6; 16:14; 18:10f.

27

theophany experienced by Elijah at Horeb[1] is a turning point. God is seen to be not only in the earthquake, wind and fire, but equally in the first low rumblings of the (political) storm; not only in the spectacular events on Carmel,[2] but in the turbulent public affairs of Israel and Syria. Yahweh's Spirit is recognized as the power of God steadily working His purpose out, and its operation is to be looked for not just in the occasional and the dramatic, but also in the humdrum affairs of every day. With the appearance of the writing prophets,[3] the steady purpose of God comes to be understood as the steady *moral* purpose of a holy and righteous God, and the Spirit as the source and mainspring of man's inner life: it is the breath of God in his nostrils that makes man a living soul,[4] and the same Spirit that alone can revitalize his moral nature. Man's true life is the life of *inspiration*, the in-breathing of God, and the prophets look forward to the time when the Spirit will be "poured out on all flesh", and men everywhere will realize their true potential.[5]

From this high water mark the tide soon began to ebb. The discovery of the lofty holiness and moral perfection of Yahweh[6] was not all gain; a high view of God's nature is always in danger of making Him remote, and it is not surprising that under the influence of Persian and Hellenistic ideas in the post-Exilic period, there was a shift of emphasis from the immanence of God, so easy and natural when He had been thought of simply as the God of Israel, to His transcendence. To this period belong the development of belief in angelic intermediaries between the holy God and

[1] I Kings 19:9ff.

[2] I Kings 18.

[3] Amos, Isaiah, Micah, etc., eighth century B.C.

[4] But not in the sense of Plato's *immortal soul*, anymore than Yahweh is I AM in the sense of Aristotle's Absolute.

[5] Joel 2:28; cf. Num. 11:29. For the deadness of man apart from the Spirit, see Ezek. 37:1ff.

[6] Isa. 6:1ff.

sinful humanity, and the personalization of God's *word* and *wisdom* as agents through whom He can deal fitly with the world of men.[1] In this climate of thought, the Spirit, previously synonymous with God Himself,[2] came to be almost a separate entity.[3]

Gradually, this separate, personalized Spirit came to be regarded as a quasi-material thing capable of being imparted by the act of anointing to selected individuals—priest, king, prophet, Messiah,[4] who then became peculiarly sacred persons. The effect of this ritual endowment of the Spirit was held to be a heightening of the individual's religious and moral consciousness so that he might the better do God's will, but nevertheless, to associate the gift of the Spirit with religious ceremonial is to widen the separation of God and the Spirit, and to encourage a materialistic view of the latter that is greatly at variance with the deeper insights of the Old Testament.

The New Testament. All four Gospels begin with a promise of the outpouring of the Spirit, and this is especially associated with the conception and birth of John the Baptist and Jesus. According to Matthew and Luke, the Holy Spirit supplied the place of a human father in the begetting of Jesus, but it is as *the power of the Highest*, not as a personalized being, that the Spirit overshadows Mary.[5] The divine action, moreover, is conditioned by human faith and obedience, and is directed towards the moral purpose of salvation. Later, at the Baptism, the Spirit descends upon Jesus in the form of a dove, but again, the accompanying words from heaven make it clear that the Spirit is not acting independently.[6] During

[1] Prov. 8; Ecclus. 1:4ff.; 24:9ff.; Wisd. 7:22.
[2] Gen. 6:3; Ps. 139:7.
[3] Isa. 48:16; Hag. 2:5.
[4] Ex. 29:7; 1 Sam. 10:1, 16:13; Isa. 61:1.
[5] Lk. 1:35.   [6] Mk. 1:10.

His Ministry, Jesus is conscious of working by the power of the Spirit, and asserts that to attribute His exorcisms (which are due to the *spirit* or *finger* of God) to demonic power, is to be guilty of blasphemy against the Spirit.[1] The Fourth Gospel presupposes Synoptic teaching, but fills out the doctrine, especially in the sayings in the Upper Room, Chapters 14 to 16. The Spirit is promised as the Advocate *Paraklētos* (AV, *Comforter*), a permanent, indwelling power that will lead the disciples into knowledge of the truth, and convict the world of sin.[2] After the Resurrection, Christ imparts the Holy Spirit to the disciples by breathing upon them, thereby empowering them to remit and retain sins. Here, too, the Spirit is still the breath or life of God.

Nowhere in the Gospels is the Spirit represented as a separate entity independent of the Father. Mt. 28:19 does suggest a distinction in the life of the Godhead, and the verse was later used as a basis for trinitarian theology, but there are good reasons for thinking that it reflects early Christian baptismal formulae rather than the actual words of Jesus.

In the Acts of the Apostles, the Holy Spirit is particularly prominent. Apart from the dramatic outpouring of the Spirit at Pentecost and at the admission of Gentiles to the Church,[3] the Spirit is seen as constantly moulding the fellowship of the Christian community and guiding its activities. The Spirit speaks, witnesses, ordains and forbids; while it does not supersede human judgment[4] nor confer infallibility, and while it can be tempted, resisted and lied against, it is the heart of the fellowship and the driving force

[1] Mt. 12:22ff.; Lk. 11:20.

[2] *Paraclete* is an exclusively Johannine term: once (1 Jn. 2:1) it refers to Christ, but in all the remaining instances (Jn. 14:16, 26; 15:26; 16:7) to the Holy Spirit.

[3] Acts 2:1–11, 10:44ff.

[4] Acts 15:28.

of the Church. There is no attempt to work out the relationship of Father, Son and Spirit, and in one place[1] the Spirit is "the spirit of Jesus". It is very obvious that the Spirit is the power of God present in the *ekklēsia*, without which not only the work of the Church, but her very existence, would be impossible.

The Pauline Epistles. The Old Testament doctrines of the Spirit as the inner principle of moral life and as the author and renewer of human nature in general, both find their fullest expression here, and especially in Romans, Corinthians (1 and 2) and Galatians. The Spirit, which comes to man through the redemption wrought by Christ and which is appropriated by faith, dwells in the believer in whom it is the source not only of peace, joy, wisdom and freedom from sin, but of the radical change that makes him a new creation, spiritual where, before, he was carnal. The emphasis is not upon occasional and startling expressions of spirit possession;[2] but on the steady impartation of those graces that build up the human personality and promote Christian fellowship.[3] As in the highest Old Testament teaching, the operation of the Spirit is to be looked for in the normal rather than the abnormal, the permanent rather than the transient. The Spirit dwells in us and we in Him, as Paul also says that we dwell in Christ and He in us, and it is this steady life in the Spirit that makes men capable of the continuous growth in grace that will bring them ever nearer to "the measure of the stature of the fulness of Christ".[4] Paul speaks of the Spirit impersonally as a power, gift or seal, but also personally as one who works, wills and can be grieved. The Apostle's interests are practical and experiential rather than theological and metaphysical,

---

[1] Acts 16:7.
[2] E.g. "speaking with tongues" (*glossolalia*).
[3] 1 Cor. 14 etc.
[4] Eph. 4:13.

and the fact of his experience is that the working of the Spirit is identical with that of the Risen Christ.[1]

2. Historical Development

The Early Church. Although, from time to time, heretics[2] denied the full divinity of the Spirit, the Church in general saw that the functions in creation and providence that Scripture attributed to the Spirit could only properly belong to one who was both personal and divine. Because the Christological controversies had made it impossible to believe in a unitary Godhead, it was unnecessary for Councils to argue the divinity of the Spirit; once the Godhead was acknowledged to comprise two Persons (Father and Son), there was no great problem in supposing it to have three. The Nicene Creed[3] speaks of the Spirit as

> The Lord and Giver of life, Who proceedeth from the Father and the Son, Who with the Father and the Son together is worshipped and glorified, Who spake by the Prophets

and seems to assert both the personality and full divinity of the Spirit, though it is not clear why some of His functions could not have been attributed either to the Father or the Son. Heretical views of the Spirit as a creature, simply one of God's ministering spirits[4] only superior to the angels, were condemned. The Spirit is not *ungenerate* like the Father (owing His existence to no external circumstance), nor

---

[1] Rom. 8:9; 2 Cor. 3:17; Eph. 3:16f.

[2] Especially the *Macedonians* of the fourth century.

[3] Often called the *Niceno-Constantinopolitan Creed*. Believed to represent the views of the Council of Nicea (A.D. 325), it was approved at Constantinople (A.D. 381) and again at Chalcedon (A.D. 451). The *filioque* ("and the Son") clause was inserted at Toledo in A.D. 447 and again in A.D. 589, and was popular in the West.

[4] Justin Martyr (*Apologia* i.6) and Tatian (*Or. adv. Graec. 13*) had held these views in the second century.

begotten like the Son; instead, He *proceeds* from Father and Son i.e. His being is contingent on theirs. Whether His procession was from the Father only, or from the Father and the Son, was the great point of dispute which led to the final breach between Eastern and Western Churches in A.D. 1054. While John 15:26 supports the Eastern or Greek position, John 16:14 favours the Western or Latin view. It is a pity that a compromise could not be reached by regarding the Spirit as proceeding *from* the Father *through* the Son.

The Reformation and After. In Protestantism, the experience of the Holy Spirit in men's hearts, confirming His testimony in the Scriptures, took the place of ecclesiastical authority and tradition. Extremes had to be guarded against. The Anabaptists claimed the Spirit's authority for the visions they had experienced, but Calvin denied this and restricted His operations to the word of Scripture, so preparing the way for a rigid biblical fundamentalism. Pietistic movements like the Moravian and the Quaker, to some extent redressed the balance, as did Roman Catholic mysticism and the early Methodist emphasis on the inner assurance of salvation, while Luther's doctrine that the Bible was the "Book of the Holy Spirit", and that the Spirit also wrote His word inwardly on the heart of the believer, left the individual free to stress *either* the authority of Scripture *or* the leading of the inward light. Where the right of private judgment is asserted, there is no easy way out of this dilemma, and the problem constantly recurs. Fortunately, this problem does not arise in the prayer and praise of the Church, and the deity of the Spirit, His operation in creation, providence and personal experience, have found beautiful poetic expression in almost every age. Notable examples are the *Odes and Psalms of Solomon*,[1] the *Quicunque Vult* (or Athanasian Creed—fifth

[1] The *Odes* probably a Christian Gnostic work, the *Psalms* Palestinian compositions of 63–60 B.C., found in some *early* Christian canons.

century), *Veni Creator Spiritus* (tenth century) and *Veni Sancte Spiritus* (thirteenth century), all but the first of which have had a tremendous influence upon Christian piety.

3. Constructive Statement

There is no doubt that Scripture speaks of the Holy Spirit's activity in personal terms, though not always consistently, and never in a way that defines the precise relationship of the Spirit to the Father and the Son. In the Old Testament, the Spirit is the Spirit of the Father, and in the New Testament that of either the Father or the Son; in both, what is meant is the immediate activity of God in individual experience and in the corporate experience of God's people. Individuals and the religious community are spirit-possessed: God is alive in them, and that is the guarantee that their faith will never be reduced to a belief in what God once did, whether in Creation or at the Incarnation. Belief that the Spirit is now at work within us safeguards God's immanence and the reality of religious experience in a way that no philosophical doctrine of God in all things (*panentheism*), or of the general dependence of matter upon mind (*subjective idealism*) ever could. While the reality of the Faith depends upon the historicity of God's redemptive acts (what God has actually *done*), it depends equally upon the present assurance in the heart and mind of the believer that He is still at work, which accounts for the frequent mention of the Spirit in the hymns and prayers of popular piety. Whether the Spirit we invoke is a manifestation of the Father's activity or of the Son's, or whether it is distinct from both, is something we do not know and which probably does not matter, as long as we know it to be divine and possessed of divine authority.

The dangers of stressing the authority of the Spirit in personal experience are obvious enough. Warm-hearted religious experience can too easily degenerate into individual licence if we have no means of testing it. Whether the spirits that we experience are of God may be open to doubt; what a man welcomes as inspiration may seem to his fellows only delusion! Catholic theology, by appealing to Church tradition, affords some criterion, while orthodox Protestantism appeals to the general tenor of the Scriptures. Mischief has occasionally been caused in both Catholic and Protestant Churches by over-zealous claims to direct, personal inspiration, but equally, in both communions, individuals have from time to time appeared in whom the Spirit was clearly at work in ways to which the orthodoxy of the time had become blind. Such religious revivals, often at the time condemned by authority, have been a periodic reminder that the Spirit has yet something to say to the Churches, and that God is still present in the midst of His people.

4

THE HOLY TRINITY

The doctrines of the Father, Son and Holy Spirit that we have traced in previous chapters had somehow or other to be reconciled with the strict monotheism that was the Church's Jewish heritage and which, rightly, it never questioned. That was the problem. Scripture and experience alike testified that God had manifested Himself in three distinct (rather than separate) modes of operation—a trinity of revelation, or *economic trinity*, and theologians concluded that He had shown Himself like that because that was what He was really like: His *nature* was three-fold. Thus the economic trinity of experience became the *essential trinity* of dogma, the doctrine that the Godhead was Triune. This doctrine, which owed its foundation to Origen,[1] was shaped in the writings of the Cappadocian Fathers (Basil, Gregory of Nazianzus, Gregory of Nyssa),[2] and found its classical expression in the fifth-century Athanasian[3] Creed, the *Quicunque Vult*.

[1] The great Alexandrian scholar, A.D. 185–255.

[2] Fourth century.

[3] So-called. Ironically, Athanasius held the Greek view, which found the divine unity in the Father, and made the Son and Spirit subordinate to Him! The *Quicunque* is certainly not the work of Athanasius (d. A.D. 373) and may even be sixth century.

1. Biblical

The term *Trinity* is not found in the New Testament, and trinitarian formulae occur in only three places:

> Go ye therefore, and make disciples of all the nations, baptizing them into the name of the Father, and of the Son and of the Holy Ghost (Mt. 28:19):

> For there are three that bear record in heaven, the Father, the Word and the Holy Ghost: and these three are one (1 Jn. 5:7):

> The grace of the Lord Jesus Christ, and the love of God, and the communion of the Holy Ghost, be with you all. (2 Cor. 13:14)

The first of these, as was said earlier, probably reflects later Church usage. The second, though printed in the Authorized Version, is not in the earliest and best manuscripts, and is omitted by the Revised Version and more recent English translations. The Corinthian passage is the classical Trinitarian text, important because it belongs to the oldest stratum of the New Testament. As we have already seen, the Gospels, Acts and Epistles furnish abundant evidence of the Church's three-fold experience of God, but the writers do not attempt detailed theological statement. That was not their purpose.

2. Historical Development

The word Trinity (Lat. *trinitas*) is first used by Tertullian (d. A.D. 240) and its Greek equivalent, Triad (*trias*) by his older contemporary, Theophilus, and, as in later usage, the terms refer to the Christian doctrine of God as Father, Son and Holy Spirit. Although notions of a divine triad occur in Indian and Egyptian religions,[1] there is no evidence that they affected Christian thought; on the other hand, Platonic ideas of the three-fold nature of Reality undoubtedly had a considerable influence in moulding Trinitarian doctrine.

[1] *Brahma—Siva—Vishnu*; *Osiris—Isis—Horus.*

Theology was trying to express the Church's experience in rational terms acceptable to contemporary philosophy, but language difficulties due to the simultaneous use of Greek and Latin, and to the absence of an agreed vocabulary, led to confusion. What was needed was some way of stating the truth that *one* God had revealed Himself in *three* modes, and that although these modes were more than *aspects* of the divine nature, they were less than self-determining personalities, for the notion of three divine egos would really be *tritheism*—belief in three gods.

The Church could not settle for that sort of polytheism, and chose instead to describe God as one substance (Gk. *ousia*, Lat. *essentia* or *substantia*) and three persons (Gk. (*hüpostasis*, Lat. *persona*), much as it described Christ as one Person with two Natures. Unfortunately, *substantia* is also the literal translation of *hüpostasis*, which had formerly been regarded as synonymous with *ousia*. To complicate matters still further, *persona* was sometimes understood as equivalent to the Gk. *prosōpon*, an actor's mask! The whole discussion was bedevilled by the fact that different writers used a common set of terms without any general agreement as to what they meant.

The modern mind would not regard *substance* as a particularly helpful way of talking about God, and *person* suggests to us a separate individual, which is not at all what the Fathers meant. The theatrical associations of *persona* and *prosōpon* were particularly unfortunate, and led some writers to regard Father, Son and Spirit as three distinct (and perhaps *successive*) rôles played by the Godhead—the heresy known as *Sabellianism*[1] or *Modalistic Monarchianism*. This heresy, popular for a time in Rome and Mesopotamia, made no great appeal to Christians generally, who were concerned to assert the *eternal* existence of Christ, but it had obvious affinities with

[1] Named after a Libyan priest, Sabellius, *c.* A.D. 200.

Docetism, Gnosticism and Patripassionism,[1] as well as with other Christological heresies like Monophysitism and Monothelitism. The opposite extreme, tritheism, while never openly avowed, was implicit in some transactional theories of the Atonement, in which redemption involved a bargain between the first and second persons of the Trinity. No doubt ordinary Christians, for whom the orthodox doctrine was too subtle, were practical tritheists, and even in modern times, the average churchman tends to think of divisions rather than distinctions in the Godhead, and to make one Person or other the object of his devotion. Thus the more intellectual, Deistic Christian worships the Father, while a more sentimental "Jesus religion" concentrates on the Son, and Pentecostal worship gives pride of place to the Spirit.

Orthodoxy, of course, insists that all three Persons are equal in majesty, glory, power and divinity, as it also affirms that the works of the Trinity are, to the outside, inseparable.[2] In acknowledging that all the Persons are incomprehensible, orthodoxy tacitly concedes that the nature of God is unknowable, and that the theological formula is used, as Augustine said, only as the alternative to silence. No man can plumb the depths of another's personality; much less can he know the secrets of the divine psychology!

Many analogies have been proposed to explain the Trinitarian mystery: the leaf of the shamrock; human intelligence, feeling and will; the lover, the beloved and the uniting bond of love (Augustine); but none is satisfactory, and most tend to Sabellianism. Despite the intellectual difficulties, the doctrine has been subscribed to (at least officially) by almost all Christians in every age. The Socinians of the

---

[1] The theory that it was *God the Father* who suffered on the Cross.

[2] There is also a doctrine that each Person exists in and permeates the others—the *perichorēsis* or *circumincessio*, a similar doctrine to the *communicatio idiomatum* (p. 28) used to explain the coinherence of the two natures in the Person of Christ.

sixteenth century and later Unitarians have denied it, but Greeks and Latins in the Early Church, the Schoolmen, and Roman Catholics and Protestants in modern times have all felt the doctrine to be essential to, or a logical inference from, the facts of revelation and experience.

3. Constructive Statement

This almost universal conviction no doubt arises from three main considerations:

(1) We cannot reasonably refer the saving work of Christ, and the power of the Holy Spirit to beings who are less than eternal, personal and divine.

(2) Something more than a unitary Godhead is implied by the biblical revelation that God's *eternal nature* is love. A unitary Godhead would have *needed* to create in order to fulfil His own personality, and creation could not have been a work of grace.

(3) God must be eternally what revelation has shown Him to be. Either God's nature is triune, or revelation has misled and deceived us.

But to say that God is, in fact, *three* and yet *one*, is to speak not of a mathematical but an *organic* trinity in unity. God is one Person to Himself, but three Persons in our experience: He who made the world was incarnate in Jesus Christ and is still at work in our hearts. To say that, is to speak of a nature quite beyond our actual experience, but as we know that the complexity of organization increases from the lower to the higher forms of life,[1] we may expect the personality of the most perfect being to exhibit the greatest complexity. It may be, indeed, that it is only the self-centred individualism of our fallen nature that makes it hard for us to grasp the nature of true life as revealed in a triune God.

[1] This, indeed, is the basis of biological classification.

40

Triune nature, as being the attribute of perfection, will, of course, be perfectly integrated, which will explain why the New Testament ascribes functions (e.g. intercession) sometimes to the Son, sometimes to the Spirit,[1] and why in experience we sometimes attribute to the risen Christ what is more appropriately attributed to the work of the Holy Spirit. As the persons of the Trinity are One God, it is not important that we should be able to say which person we are dealing with at any given time.

In any case, what we can know of the divine Nature is only indirectly and by inference: we cannot "fathom the mystery of God" nor "fathom the perfection of the Almighty".[2] Only the *economic trinity* is present to experience and immediately discoverable in Scripture. For practical purposes, that is enough: we are to "pray to the Father, through the Son, in the Holy Ghost".[3] If the doctrine of the Trinity helps us to do that, it is as much as most of us will ask.

[1] cf. Jn. 11:42; Heb. 9:24; Rom. 8:26.
[2] Job 11:7 (NEB).
[3] Origen.

PART TWO

THE DOCTRINES OF MAN, SIN AND SALVATION

5

MAN AND SIN

1. Biblical

Man. The starting point is that man is a creature made by God. Like the other animals, he is made of ordinary chemical elements—the dust of the earth—and like them he is a living creature because he possesses the breath of God, which is what the living have and the dead lack. He is not a being in his own right—his existence, like that of the animals, is contingent upon God;[1] God has given man and the animals life, and if He should withhold His breath they will die. So far man is like the rest of the animals, but *unlike* them, he is made in the image and likeness of God, which means that, like God and unlike the animals, man is a responsible being capable of moral choice. Man may not blame his short-comings on his animal nature, for he is put in charge of the lower creatures: he gives the animals their names,[2] that is, allots their place and functions. Man determines them, they do not determine him.

But despite his moral freedom and extensive powers,[3] despite the radical distinction between man and the other animals which must at all costs be preserved,[4] man is not God,

[1] Job 34:14f.; Ps. 104:29f.; Acts 17:24, 28.
[2] Gen. 2:19.
[3] Ps. 8.   [4] Lev. 18:23; 20:15.

as his disastrous attempt to usurp divine authority will prove. Man is flesh, and indeed, *all flesh* is a common biblical description of humanity in general, or even of all living creatures. Not that man is the worse for being flesh: Hebrew thought does not regard the physical as inferior to the spiritual, much less as evil in itself. It is simply that God is Creator and man a creature, and again there is a distinction to be observed.[1]

Man in the biblical sense is the *race* of men, for Adam is the Hebrew not only for a human individual, but for humanity as a whole. All men have a common ancestry,[2] and though there is a multiplicity of nations, and soon a confusion of tongues,[3] all share the common flesh, and all are truly men. Israel is the chosen people, and his *election* is an important factor in Old Testament religion, but like creation itself, it is an act of sovereign grace. It is not that Israel is more human or more deserving,[4] only that he is chosen to be the special possession of God, and to play a missionary rôle among the nations.[5] All nations have a place within the divine scheme of things, even if Jewish exclusiveness sometimes forgot that.

Individually, too, man is a unity; the Bible may speak of bones, flesh, heart etc. as the locations of thought, feeling, will, but the individual is thought of as a totality, and only as he possesses an inner harmony is he truly human. This true humanity is always in a social context; man is a member of his group and enjoys a solidarity with it. In that sense, man can never be viewed in isolation from his fellows, and the Bible therefore takes the social aspects of man more seriously than we can, who place too much stress on personal freedom and responsibility. To punish the group for the sin of its member[6]

---

[1] Job 33:12ff.; Ps. 103:14ff.; Isa. 55:8f.; Hos. 11:9.
[2] Gen. 5:1–6.1; cf. Acts. 17:26; 1 Cor. 15:39.
[3] Gen. 11.
[4] Deut. 7:7f.; 10:14, 15, 19; Ps. 67:2ff.
[5] Isa. 49:4, 6, 7.
[6] Jos. 22:20.

is not, to the ancient Hebrew mind, gross injustice, but a recognition of the natural order of things.[1] Man cannot be abstracted from his social context without ceasing to be a whole man, nor can he be taken out of his original relationship with God, without becoming less than he was intended to be.

But in fact, man is always less than God intended because he is a sinner alienated from, and in rebellion against, his Maker. The origin of sin is never formally discussed, but there is no doubt that the early chapters of Genesis speak

> Of Man's first disobedience, and the fruit
> Of that forbidden tree whose mortal taste
> Brought death into the World, and all our woe,
> With loss of Eden. . . .[2]

Though no clear-cut doctrine is developed, it is plain enough to see the connection between the revolt of man (Gen. 3) and the angels (Gen. 6) and the appalling moral chaos that follows. From the abuse of free will flows a general confusion: the perversion of Nature (Gen. 3:14ff.), strife among the nations (Gen. 11), and a degenerate spiritual condition, described in the words of Gen. 6:5:

> And the Lord saw that the wickedness of man was great in the earth, and that every imagination of the thoughts of his heart was only evil continually.[3]

Created by God as part of a work that was good, man quickly fell from grace, but there is no coherent doctrine of a Fall. The Eden story is not referred to again in the Old Testament,[4]

---

[1] Later, the Prophets were a good deal more individualistic: cf. Jer. 31:29f.; Ezek. 3 and 18.

[2] *Paradise Lost*, I:1ff.

[3] For a similar NT view of human depravity, see Rom. 1:18ff.

[4] The *garden*, Eden, is mentioned in Isa. 51:3; Joel 2:3, while Ezek. 28:13ff. may refer to an Adamic Fall.

and the fall of angels only doubtfully in Isaiah 14:12ff. Jesus mentions man's creation once,[1] but only in connection with the indissolubility of marriage, and when Paul talks of Adam's Fall and its consequences,[2] he does it to stress the redemptive power of Christ rather than to say how sin originated.

In late post-Exilic Judaism, however, there was considerable speculation about the Fall. Human sinfulness was sometimes attributed to Adam's disobedience,[3] sometimes to the revolt of the angels,[4] and sometimes, as in Hebrew fragments of Ecclesiasticus, to an all-pervasive evil influence or *yezer ha-ra'*.[5] By Christian times, an Adamic Fall theory probably held the field in rabbinic Judaism though human pride being what it is, popular theology no doubt preferred to attribute man's wrong-doing to the external influence of demons than to any inborn taint. Both biblical and post-biblical teaching accepted the reality of free will; whatever Adam may have done, man still sinned voluntarily—"Each man has become the Adam of his own soul."[6]

Sin. The ordinary Hebrew and Greek words used in the Old and New Testaments make plain the nature of sin: it is failure (missing the mark), it is perversion or crookedness, but more importantly it is rebellion—man in revolt. Whatever the personal and social consequences of sin, its worst aspect is that it is an affront to God, which is the justification for Psalm 51:4:

> Against thee, thee only, have I sinned, and done that which is evil in thy sight.

[1] Mk. 10:6ff.

[2] Rom. 5:12ff.

[3] 2 Esdr. 7:46ff.

[4] With NT echoes in 1 Cor. 11:10; Jude 6f.; 2 Pet. 1:4; 2:4.

[5] This doctrine is also prominent in the Qumrân texts or *Dead Sea Scrolls.*

[6] *Apocalypse of Baruch,* 54:19.

45

Because sin breaks the ordained relationship between man and his Creator, all sin affects God.

That is why sacrifice for sin is so prominent in the Old Testament. A common crime like theft, for instance, is not only a crime but sin: it can never be a private matter between the thief and his victim. When restitution has been made, and the fine paid, the guilt offering (*asham*) is required.[1] At its highest, of course, Old Testament teaching stressed that the alienated sinner could be restored only by God's free pardon, and the emphasis in the Prophets is on God's covenant-love pardoning sinners rather than on the efficacy of the sacrificial system which, in any case, was regularly concerned with ritual offences that we should hardly call sin.

Jesus certainly accepts the universality of sin—"You, then, being evil"—[2] but in the Gospels and throughout the New Testament, it is the *spiritual condition* of sin rather than the detailing of specific wrong acts that is important. The spiritual state (not unlike the *hübris*—arrogance—that is a recurring theme of Greek tragedy) is what matters, and the deadly sins are the pride and self-righteousness typified by the Pharisee, not the sensual sins of the lower orders.[3]

2. Historical Development

It was the Atonement that first focused the Church's attention on sin, and that should always be kept in mind: however harsh some of the judgments on man's state, they are made in the context of Christ's redemptive activity. The gospel preached was a gospel of salvation, and the problem of sin was always seen in relation to the remedy that God had provided in the death and Resurrection of Jesus. The first preaching[4]

[1] Lev. 6:1–7.
[2] Mt. 7:11.
[3] Lk. 18:9ff.
[4] Acts 2:14ff.; 3:13ff.; 10:34ff.; 13:16ff.

never started, in reverse order, with human sin but always with the saving initiative of God in Christ.

At various times there were, however, some attempts to classify sin. The Catholic tradition drew a distinction between *mortal* and *venial* (less serious) sin, a distinction rejected by Protestant theologians, who held that, since all sin was sin against God, all sin was grave. Scholars have spoken of *formal* sin—where the sinner acts against conscience, even if the thing done is right, and *material* sin—thoughts, words and deeds which are in fact contrary to the will of God, whether the sinner knows it or not. Again, theologians have argued whether sin is a negative thing (*privatio*)—the absence of righteousness, or *depravatio*—positive wickedness. Those who have taken the latter view have then had to consider whether the sinner is totally depraved, so that the image of God is quite effaced, or whether the resulting depravity is only partial— the image defaced but not entirely lost.

Granted that man was created in the image of God, that likeness must somehow have been blurred or obliterated, and this change for the worse in man has generally been attributed to a Fall, and usually to a Fall of Adam rather than of the angels.[1] Unfortunately, through the influence of Augustine of Hippo (whose besetting sin before conversion, was lust), sin has often been thought of in an altogether too narrow way as concupiscence: that is a pity, for the root of sin is *pride* rather than desire. It is also a pity that we do not know man *before* the Fall: was he immortal and supernaturally endowed "the perfect athlete, philosopher and saint",[2] or was he (as the Genesis narrative suggests) mortal, simple and innocent? If there was a Fall, did God *will* it (by a divine decree), or did He only *foresee* it? If He decreed it, was the

[1] The best English account of theories of the Fall is by N. P. Williams, *The Ideas of the Fall and of Original Sin.*

[2] Cf. R. South (1634–1716): *An Aristotle was but the rubbish of an Adam and Athens but the rudiments of Paradise—Sermons*, Vol. 1.i.

decree *prior* to the Fall (*supralapsarianism*), or *subsequent* to it (*infralapsarianism*)? Whatever the timing, was the decree one that destined some men to be saved, or was there double predestination, assigning some men to damnation? These are some of the questions that Churchmen debated, and we must now look at the more important positions that they adopted.

Augustine of Hippo (354–430). In his paradisal state, man was possessed of super-human intellect, immunity from pain and immortal youth. The first sin caused the Fall which made man mortal, and though it did not abolish free will, its entail (*Original Sin*) passed to all men by biological inheritance, and humanity can be regarded as a "lump of sin" (*massa peccati*). Original Sin carries with it *original guilt*, and therefore unbaptized infants, if they die, go to hell. In that case, the infant is not punished unjustly; like the rest of us, he is properly guilty of what he cannot help! Not only human sinfulness, but all the woes of life, including what we should call "acts of God", are due to the Fall.

In effect, Augustine divides mankind into three groups.
(1) There are those whom God elects in eternity, and calls in time to be "vessels of grace". These have the gifts of *efficacious grace* and perseverance, and go ultimately to heaven. This is God's mercy.
(2) There are some whom God predestines to membership of the Church, but as these lack the gift of perseverance, they slip back into the "damned mass" and are finally lost.
(3) This "damned mass" is the rest of mankind, who, though given *sufficient grace*, always reject it and gravitate to hell. This is justice, for the damned have rejected grace.

Augustine does not say definitely that God *predestines* some men to damnation, but that they are left to it—and the moral distinction is a fine one!

Sin, according to Augustine, is *defect* (absence of good), a notion that does not fit particularly well with some of his other views. Again, *total depravity* (the doctrine that man is utterly corrupt) is not asserted, but as the unbaptized are incapable of good, it is clearly implied. God always foreknows what response any individual will make to his circumstances, but man still chooses, so that his punishment, when it comes, is deserved. On the other hand, the elect do not merit election —that is sheer grace, though of course, being elect, they do good works.

Augustine's system really represents Pauline teaching on sin and grace carried to its logical conclusion, and it is almost impossible to exaggerate its influence on Western theology.

Pelagius (*fl. c.* 400), a British monk was, with his disciple, Coelestius, Augustine's chief opponent. Technically a heretic, Pelagius's views modified some of the sterner aspects of Augustine's teaching, and a resultant *semi-Pelagianism* became widely held, especially among Franciscans (see Duns Scotus, below) and Jesuits. Pelagius taught that Adam was created *mortal*, and would have died even if he had not sinned. In fact, Adam did sin, but his sin affected only himself, so there is no room for original sin *or* original guilt. Man is free and can be sinless if he chooses: there were sinless men before Christ— the Law, as well as the Gospel, leads to the Kingdom. Augustine's teaching about infants was completely rejected; even if unbaptized, they have eternal life.

Pelagianism represents the popular, over-simple form of Christian theology (what has been called "the once-born" type), and its refreshingly commonsense statements had immense appeal. Its strength was that it allowed real free will, and insisted that God's justice must be taken seriously. Its weakness was that it did not really face up to the *universal* sinfulness of mankind. Despite Pelagius, "No man is an island . . ."!

Anselm (1033–1109), Archbishop of Canterbury, and one of the earliest of the Schoolmen,[1] tried to combine Augustinianism with the possibility of human merit, which seemed to be required by the Church's penitential system. According to Anselm, man's freedom is only *impaired* by original sin, and because the sin of infants cannot involve the will, it is not deserving of punishment. Sin is dishonouring God, and the sinner ought to make restitution, but in fact, the works of the penitent (though He does not condemn them) are not sufficient to merit salvation.

Peter Abelard (1079–1142) held that sin lies in the intention, and therefore the sin of ignorance is not properly sin. Abelard could not believe that God would damn a man for the sin of his parents, and consequently he denied original guilt.

Duns Scotus (1270–1308), a Franciscan, held a modified Augustinianism. Before the Fall, Adam had only a *provisional* righteousness and immortality. After the Fall, man's will was still free, and even without grace, men (including pagans) can do works of which God approves. The problem of predestination *versus* free will is tackled by suggesting that there is a harmony between the eternal decrees and the results of human choice, so that evil cannot simply be blamed on God as it must be, surely, on Augustine's view. Original sin is thought of as only the lack of original righteousness, and physical desire is not itself sinful. Unbaptized infants have a pleasant and soothing existence in Limbo. Oddly, Duns Scotus retained original guilt, but probably only from fear of being branded a Pelagian.

Thomas Aquinas (1226–74) was a Dominican friar[2] whose

---

[1] Medieval philosophers and theologians, so-called from their tendency to form distinct *schools* of thought.

[2] Aquinas's system is known as *Thomism*.

massive work the *Summa Theologica* became the classic exposition of Catholic teaching. Aquinas combined Christian theology with Aristotelian philosophy, and his system represents the height of Scholasticism. He accepts predestination and reprobation, but this combines with free will, and leaves room for merit; on his view, man does voluntarily what is predestined. At the Creation, man had human nature as such, plus an inclination to virtue and a *super-added gift* of grace. The Fall resulted in the loss of original righteousness, and the withdrawal of grace. Adam's sin was pride, and fallen man shows his state *materially* in inordinate desire, and *formally* in lack of original righteousness. These make up original sin and its accompanying guilt. Double predestination is accepted; the reprobate receive *sufficient* grace of which, in fact, they never avail themselves, while the elect have *efficacious grace*, which is irresistible. Sin is *defect*, and since it cannot have been made, God cannot be responsible for it.

The Council of Trent, which met intermittently from 1545–63, attempted to lay down a common, acceptable theological statement in an age when Protestantism was menacing a Roman Church already torn by internal disputes, and its Articles[1] are still the basis of orthodox Roman theology.

The Council affirmed that man was *constituted* in original righteousness, and that by the Fall, Adam *changed for the worse*. That is original sin, and it is universal. Man's free will was weakened and biased by the Fall, but it was not extinguished. Concupiscence is not really sin. Merit is due to the *infusion* of divine grace, but always requires man's co-operation.

In a sense, Trent was a struggle between the Dominicans on the one hand, and the Franciscans and Jesuits on the other. The Articles of the Council were a compromise; original guilt was retained, but free will was strongly affirmed, and room was found for the good works of non-Christians.

[1] Sometimes called the *Tridentine* Decrees.

Neither side won a complete victory, and the theology of the Council may be fairly described as semi-Pelagian or semi-Augustinian, according to preference!

The Reformation and After

John Calvin (1509–64). Calvinism is always popularly associated with the doctrine of predestination though in fact, that doctrine is only part of John Calvin's teaching,[1] and a part moreover, that is primarily intended to express man's utter dependence on the *grace of God*, and the impossibility that men should ever earn salvation.

According to Calvin, sin is not just absence of virtue, but a positive corruption inherited from Adam, whose sin was *apostasy*—turning from God. The depravity of man affects the whole of his being, and in that sense is total, but Calvin still allows the virtue of the unregenerate as Augustine did not. Election, either to salvation or damnation, is by *eternal divine decree* and is quite independent of human merit. The hardest things that Calvin said were the result of remorseless logic: if an infant has Original Sin, then its state must be abhorrent to a God who hates sin!

The followers of Calvin disagreed about whether the object of the divine decree was man *created and fallen*, or man *about to be created and liable to fall*. The latter view, held by Beza, Calvin's successor, is called *supralapsarianism*; the opposite, more moderate *infralapsarianism*, was championed by Bullinger, and became generally held by Calvinist churches.

Jacobus Arminius (1560–1609). The main opposition to Calvinism came from this Dutchman, who attacked predestination as a doctrine that made God the author of sin.

[1] *Institutes of the Christian Religion*; first published in French (1539), it attained its final form in the Latin edition of 1559. A massive, lucid and readable work which has had immense influence on Protestant thought.

After Arminius's death, his followers drew up the *Remonstrance* (1610), which denied *supra-* and *infralapsarianism*, the restriction of the benefits of Christ's Passion to the elect, irresistible grace, and the indefectibility of the saints.[1] On the positive side, Arminians asserted that Christ died *for all men*, and saves all who believe.

The Anglican Church (*Articles of Religion*, 1562)[2] and the Presbyterian Churches (*Westminster Confession*, 1643) are officially Calvinist in their doctrines of sin and grace; the Methodist Church is Arminian. In practice, the distinction is blurred; as has been wisely said, we all tend to be Calvinists on our knees, Arminians in the pulpit!

3. Constructive Statement

The discussion about man's original state, and the arguments about the divine decrees, are fruitless: we know nothing from Scripture or experience about either. We do know about the uneasy conscience of man in every age, and the universality of sin certainly demands an explanation. It is, in fact, harder to be good than bad, and even small children appear to have a propensity for cruelty and wickedness. Again, we feel shame for what we know we cannot wholly help (e.g. alcoholism), and because of social ties, we suffer and feel guilt for the sins of our group.

While we do not understand enough about inherited characteristics to speak with confidence, we do know that spiritually as well as mentally we are in some sense what our forebears have made us. There seems to be a corporate sinful-

[1] The impossibility that the elect should sin and fall away—a doctrine found both in Augustine and Calvin.

[2] The *Articles* have been held (esp. by Anglo-Catholics) to be capable of a Catholic interpretation. The Church of England is not easy to classify, and in some respects is Protestant, in others Catholic; Anglicans themselves vary widely on these points.

ness, a solidarity in sin, which must have a cause; man is clearly not what an all-good Creator would have wished, and some sort of Fall appears to be required by the evidence. The doctrines of original sin and original guilt (especially the former) find echoes in present experience. It is, of course, possible to believe in original sin without believing that it involves guilt, and some theologians have adopted that position. Another possibility is to believe that we have only corporate, not personal, responsibility for the sin of the race.

Old attempts to classify sin are not particularly helpful, but nor are modern attempts[1] to explain sin as an imbalance of instincts, e.g. by saying that man has too much *self-regarding* and too little *herd* instinct. Again, we cannot be content with the view of F. R. Tennant[2] who, like Pelagius and many Liberal Protestants, limits sin to deliberate wrong-doing. As Cave[3] points out, sin is primarily a *religious*, not an ethical concept, and we need forgiveness for what we *are*, as well as for what we *do*!

Man is too complex a creature for any single explanation of his imperfect state, whether in simple biological,[4] economic[5] or psychological[6] terms. Last century's optimistic view of man as gradually evolving from primitive beginnings towards ultimate perfection (falling upwards!), is untenable in times that have seen the horrors that can be perpetrated by civilized nations: the blemish which the Bible and theologians call sin, is an obstinate fact of life. But it is not the *only* fact of life; if there is sin, there is also, in Christ, full salvation, and it is to this that we must now turn.

---

[1] E.g. N. P. Williams, *Ideas of the Fall and Original Sin.*

[2] *The Origin and Propagation of Sin* (1901–2); *The Concept of Sin* (1912).

[3] S. Cave, *The Christian Estimate of Man* (1944), p. 186.

[4] Remnants of the ape and the tiger not yet discarded.

[5] The Marxist view.

[6] Especially Sigmund Freud. It is interesting that as Augustine and others linked *sin* with sexuality, so many moderns explain *guilt* by it!

6

SALVATION

1. Biblical

Because the worst aspect of sin is the broken relationship with God, its remedy is the restoration of fellowship (at-one-ment), and in that, God takes the initiative; man is to be reconciled to God, for it is man that is alienated, not God. At one level, the Old Testament may be described as the record of God's mighty acts of deliverance from external enemies, hunger, pestilence and so forth; at another level, it is the story of the redemptive activity of God in saving men from sin, and at both levels the divine activity is the exercise of sovereign grace —the steady love of a God who keeps covenant.

God does not infuse or bestow His grace to make men better than they are, and fit to be pardoned. He shows His grace by *putting away* or *not remembering* the sin, by justifying men simply on condition of their trust in Him. To *justify* is not to make just, nor even to pronounce just, but to *treat as just*. The opposite of giving a dog a bad name and hanging him is to give him a good name and save him, and that is precisely what God does to man. Man does not become righteous by faith and repentance; he is treated as righteous and then gradually becomes so, as by divine help, he begins to live up to the status he does not deserve. Paul brings out the enormity of this in the pungent phrase about "justifying the ungodly".[1] Quite obviously, salvation has nothing to do with the operation of justice, and everything to do with the exercise of the prerogative of mercy. Were God bound by the laws of justice, justice would be greater than He.

So, Abraham is treated as righteous simply because he trusts God. It is not that Abraham is *made* righteous by trusting God —only that, once trust is established, Abraham is in the *right relationship*[2] with God, which is really what the Bible means by righteousness. For that matter, it is the restoration of relationships, rather than any consideration of justice, that is the essence of human reconciliation. In Pauline language, righteousness is the *righteousness of faith*, sharply contrasted with the (self) righteousness that men try to attain by moral effort and the cultivation of virtue. The relationship is all-important; just as man sins because he is a sinner (not *vice versa*), man becomes a saint because he is saved, and not the other way round.

The saving initiative of God is shown in the Law and Covenant and in the Prophets. In the Law, the stress is upon giving God His place:[3] that is where the Ten Commandments begin, and the moral conduct demanded by the last six "words" follows from it. Again, the Covenant is made by God, not negotiated by man, and so is the new, more inward covenant envisaged by Jeremiah[4] and Ezekiel.[5] Even the sacrificial system, in which men *appear* so active, is given by God; it is not a means devised by man for propitiating His anger.

It is true that, at a cursory reading, the Prophets sometimes

[1] Rom. 4:5.

[2] The root meaning of the Hebrew words for salvation, *yeshuah*, *yesha*, *teshuah*, is *spaciousness*—"to be unconfined", "to be at ease"—an ideal that we may contrast with the restrictive, cramping effect of shame and guilt.

[3] Not as Despot, but as Saviour, *Deliverer* (Ex. 20:1).

[4] Jer. 31:31ff.

[5] Ezek. 37:26ff.

appear to speak as though, by mending his ways, man might aspire to save himself,[1] but closer study shows that every moral exhortation is in the context of God's redemptive activity: indeed, God would hardly have sent the Prophets, had the initiative not been with Him. Salvation history is the chronicle of God's repeated appeals to the sinner, as Jesus makes very plain in the parable of the Wicked Husbandmen.[2]

Indeed, the New Testament takes up the story and adds another chapter to the chronicle. God's Son is called *Jesus* because *He shall save His people from their sins*,[3] and the Incarnation can be summed up in Jn. 3:16 in terms of the Father's saving purpose for His world, as it is also in 2 Cor. 5:19—"God was in Christ reconciling the world unto Himself". But as the New Testament is silent about the nature of the Divine/human union in Christ's person, so it offers no theory of His atoning work. Jesus saves, but New Testament writers do not tell us how He saves, except that the redemptive work is through His suffering, death and Resurrection.

Jesus refers to His life as "a ransom for many",[4] and at the Last Supper speaks of the New Covenant in His own blood,[5] while His followers see His sufferings in terms of the suffering servant of Isaiah 53.[6] Again, Paul talks of Jesus as the *last Adam*, undoing the mischief of the first man,[7] and in Philippians 2:5-11 brings together both last Adam and suffering servant ideas. The nearest that the New Testament comes to a coherent doctrine of the Work of Christ is in the Epistle to the Hebrews, where Calvary is seen in the light of the Jewish sacrificial cultus, and Christ is represented as at once priest and victim,

[1] Mic. 6:8; Amos 5:14f.; Isa. 58:6ff.
[2] Mk. 12:1ff.
[3] Mt. 1:21.
[4] Mk. 10:45.
[5] Mk. 14:23f.
[6] Acts 3:13, 26; 4:27, 30; 1 Pet. 2:22–25.
[7] 1 Cor. 15:21f., 45; cf. Rom. 5:19.

offering the perfect, once-for-all atonement that the old dispensation was powerless to effect.[1] Illuminating and suggestive as these and other passages are, they do not amount to a finished theory. What is very clear indeed is that all the New Testament writers saw the life, death and Resurrection of Jesus as the fulfilment of God's saving purpose, and as the remedy for man's sin: beyond that, they have nothing to say.

2. Historical Development

Unlike the doctrine of the Person of Christ, the Work of Christ has never been the subject of conciliar decision, and adherence to a particular theory of the Atonement has not been made a test of orthodoxy: so long as a Christian could subscribe to the quite general statements contained in the Creeds, nothing further was required of him. That is not to say that the doctrine of the Work of Christ has not been the subject of serious speculation throughout the centuries. Theologians in every age have wrestled with the problem, and the developed soteriologies that they have worked out have been of four main types:

> The Classical, Dramatic or Patristic
> The Juridical or (in some forms) Penal Substitutionist
> The Subjectivist or Moral Influence Theory
> The Representative or Sacrificial Theory.

Of these, all but the third are *objective* or *transactional* theories, emphasizing what God in Christ *did*, while the subjectivist theory stresses the moral effect on the believer. Broadly, it may also be said that the three objective theories really deal with the removal of guilt (what theologians call *reatus*), the other theory with the eradication of sin (*vitium*), though neither of these distinctions can be rigidly maintained.

The Classical, Dramatic or Patristic Theory, which has been

[1] E.g. Heb. 7:27.

advanced in various forms from time to time, has been persuasively restated in the present century by G. Aulén.[1] Irenaeus, Bishop of Lyons (*fl.* A.D. 180), at one point[2] put forward a *Recapitulation* theory—that Christ summed up human history in Himself, regaining for man what had been lost in Adam, a view that accords quite well with Rom. 5:18f. In a later passage of the same work,[3] Irenaeus speaks of Christ's death as ransoming man from the Devil.

It was ransom theories, common in the Patristic period, that Gregory of Nazianzus attacked as *monstrous* if the ransom was regarded as paid by God to the Devil, and *unnecessary* if paid by the Son to the Father! Despite Gregory's strictures, ransom theories had a natural appeal in an age of brigandage, and largely held the field until Anselm.

Properly stated (e.g. by Bishop Aulén) as a victory over evil, the Classical Theory emphasizes the once-for-allness of the atoning act, and because it is victory that is in mind, stresses Resurrection equally with Crucifixion. Another strength of the theory is that the extent and power of evil in the world is faced squarely; but it is difficult to account satisfactorily for the persistence of sin so long after victory has been won.

The Juridical or Satisfactionist Theory of Anselm,[4] in line with notions of medieval chivalry, saw the Atonement as a satisfaction offered to God's wounded honour—a satisfaction that man owed, but only the sinless Christ could offer. On this theory, Jesus Christ, *as man, bore the penalty of man's sin,* and offered satisfaction in our stead.[5]

The theory fits well enough with 1 Pet. 3:18: "Christ also suffered for sins once, the righteous for the unrighteous, that he might bring us to God", but it does put rather too much

---

[1] *Christus Victor* (1931).

[2] *Adv. Haer.* III, xviii.

[3] V, i.1.

[4] *Cur Deus Homo?* I and II.

[5] Cf. *There was no other good enough to pay the price of sin.*

stress on the rôle played by Christ's manhood. Protestants have tended to adopt *Penal Substitutionist* forms of the theory —Christ bearing the *penalty* of sin that should have been man's,[1] a notion which, though it can be defended as less than grotesque injustice,[2] does raise very real difficulties. How can Christ *really* substitute for man, and even if He can, why should God inflict an arbitrary punishment on the innocent when, presumably, He could waive it? Theories of this kind are not attractive in an age that believes in personal responsibility, but they have some scriptural support in the Isaianic doctrine of the servant's vicarious suffering, and fit our own experience of a world in which the innocent all too often suffer for the guilty.

The Subjectivist, Abelardian or Moral Influence Theory, advanced in the medieval period by Peter Abelard and Peter Lombard, was revived in the modern age by Horace Bushnell and Hastings Rashdall,[3] and proved popular with Liberal Protestants. According to this view, the Cross is a manifestation of God's *eternal* suffering love, and evokes a moral response in man, leading him to penitence and amendment of life.

This theory, which reflects some New Testament texts, is true enough; what Christ did *for* us objectively on the Cross must have a subjective influence *in* us if it is to be effective at all. The fatal flaw is that the theory is based upon an inadequate assessment of the extent and gravity of sin, and that it evades the question of what it was that Christ *did*.

The Sacrificial or Representative Theory, persuasively stated by Dr. Vincent Taylor,[4] leans heavily upon the Epistle to the

[1] Cf. *Bearing shame and scoffing rude/In my place condemned He stood.*

[2] E.g. in modern times, by R. W. Dale, E. Brunner.

[3] H. Bushnell, *The Vicarious Sacrifice* (1877); H. Rashdall, *The Idea of the Atonement in Christian Theology* (1919).

[4] *Jesus and His Sacrifice* (1937); *The Atonement in NT Teaching* (1940); *Forgiveness and Reconciliation* (1941).

Hebrews. As in Old Testament sacrifice (at its best) the sinner becomes identified with the sinless victim[1] so the sinner is identified with Christ, who is our Representative. As our Representative, Christ offers to God the perfect sacrifice that man cannot offer: only a sinless man can experience complete penitence, for he only can understand the enormity of sin.

While this theory is perhaps the greatest modern attempt to construct an acceptable doctrine of Atonement, it has been criticized as adopting too favourable a view of Old Testament sacrifice, and[2] as making God require of men a perfect penitence, whereas, on the Pauline and Protestant view, salvation is conditional only on *faith*.

3. Constructive Statement

The brief account that we have given of the great Atonement theories is an outline rather than a picture, and cannot do them justice. Massive intellects have wrestled with the problems of sin and salvation, and every theory that has been advanced contains some germ of truth, if none is by itself, completely satisfactory. The several theories are complementary, and each contains some elements of the others; if the deeper insights of any of the four were lost, Christian theology would be immeasurably the poorer.

The simplest theory, Abelard's, brings out the fact that God loved before, as well as after Calvary, and stresses the eternal nature of redemption, but it does not do justice to the uniqueness of the Christ-event. Something new and dramatic happened on Good Friday and Easter Day, and that something neither Abelard nor his great disciple, Peter Lombard, really

[1] All sacrificial victims had to be unblemished; the only animal *bearer* of sin (the Scapegoat) was *not* sacrificed.
[2] By Dr. N. H. Snaith.

made clear. The theory is good and necessary as far as it goes, but it does not go far enough.[1]

The oldest theories, the Classic or Patristic, have their own special merit. Man *is* in bondage to sin and evil, and there is a price to be paid for his redemption. To ask "to whom is the ransom paid, to God or the Devil?" is to press a useful metaphor too far, and to suggest (as Gregory of Nazianzus did) that God could have remitted the penalty unless the principle of justice were greater than He, is altogether too facile. In a moral universe, God could not minimize the *cost* of salvation, for that would be to heal the hurt of sin too lightly. The virtue of satisfactionist and penal theories is that they reckon with the gravity of sin and recognize the costliness of salvation. In the more developed *Christus Victor* form, the Classic theory brings out the element of struggle and victory in the Passion of Jesus, and presents the Crucifixion and Resurrection as a single, dramatic confrontation with the powers of evil. We all know in experience something of the extent of evil, and moral effort is always war against its thrall. If evil lingers on, we believe it to have been defeated in principle; whatever else the events of Holy Week mean, they do mean victory, and it is a merit of this theory to make that quite clear.

The Sacrificial or Representative theory, by its positive identification of the sinner with the sinless Son of Man (and Son of God), who offers in man's name the supreme sacrifice of obedience, love and penitence, preserves the more valuable insights of Recapitulation and Satisfactionist theories in a form free from some of the most telling objections against them. Not least among the merits of Dr. Taylor's theory is that it provides a soteriological background for our belief in effective faith-union with Christ, and lends an additional

[1] Dr. N. H. Snaith thinks the theory satisfactory *provided the moral influence is seen as a work of the Holy Spirit in the heart.* (Private communication)

dimension to sacramental devotion. No doubt that explains why the theory has appealed both to Protestants and Roman Catholics.

Preoccupation with questions of Christology no doubt prevented the Church's probing too far into the nature of the Atonement; sufficient that Christ "suffered also for us under Pontius Pilate", and that we can affirm our belief in "the forgiveness of sins". Exactly what it was that Christ did on the Cross, we shall never know. That He died "for us men and for our salvation", we can never doubt, and that is both the kernel of the Gospel and the basis of Church life and personal devotion.

PART THREE

THE DOCTRINES OF CHURCH, MINISTRY AND SACRAMENTS

7

THE CHURCH

1. Biblical

Although the Church (Gk. *ekklēsia*) is a specifically Christian institution and therefore belongs quite definitely to the New Testament, its roots are certainly in old Israel, for it signifies the New Testament People of God as clearly as the Hebrew words *edhah* (congregation) and *qahal* (assembly) denote the People of God in earlier times. Israel, chosen by Yahweh as His own peculiar treasure,[1] was to be a missionary agent:

> Ye shall be a peculiar treasure unto me from among all peoples . . .
> And ye shall be unto me *a kingdom of priests*, and an holy nation.
> (Ex. 19:5f.)

This was in confirmation of the promise made to Abraham:

> In thy seed shall all the nations of the earth be blessed: because thou hast obeyed my voice. (Gen. 22:18)

Israel was to be the temporal instrument of Yahweh's eternal redemptive purpose; election was for service, not privilege, and that is as true of the Church as it ever was of the Israelites. The basis of Israel's election was the covenant made with Abraham and ratified with Moses (at Sinai), so Israel is not only the *chosen* people, but the *covenant* people. What Israel

[1] Heb. *segullah*.

was in the Old Testament then, the Church is in the New Testament, and that is very clear both in language and symbolism.

As to language, the word *ekklēsia* had no gentile religious connections: to the pagan Greek it meant simply an assembly of citizens called out from their homes to transact municipal business; but to the Hellenistic Jew reading the scriptures in the Septuagint version,[1] it was familiar as the Greek word for the People of God, the spiritual nation of Israel, and it is so used in the New Testament in Acts 7:38 and Heb. 2:12. *Ekklēsia* never had the narrower connotation of the local Jewish religious organization; the Septuagint word for that, and the ordinary word in the Hellenistic world, was *sünagōgē*, which the Christians always avoided. By the choice of *ekklēsia* as the designation of the body of disciples, the first Christians were expressing a sense of continuity with the Old Testament, and seeing themselves as the properly constituted gathering of all the New Israel,[2] constituted by the New Covenant as surely as old Israel was by the Covenant of Sinai.[3] Both were constituted by God, not instituted by man, and as He was present in fire on the mountain (Ex. 19:18), so His Spirit was present in fire in the upper room at Jerusalem (Acts 2:3). This identification with the true Israel is indicated not only in the continued use of *ekklēsia*, but also in New Testament references to Christians as in *the circumcision*,[4] and in the use of such metaphors as *vine* and *bride*, now used of the Church as once they were used of Israel,[5] while the number of the Disciples clearly recalls the twelve tribes of the Jews.

[1] Where it invariably translates *qahal*. *Sünagōgē* was used mostly for *edhah*, only rarely for *qahal*.

[2] Gal. 3:16; cf. Rom. 9 and 11.

[3] Dr. Snaith, in a personal communication, makes the interesting suggestion that *ekklēsia* may have been adopted partly because it *sounded* like *qahal*.

[4] Phil. 3:3; Col. 2:11.

[5] Isa. 5:7; Hos. 2:2; cf. Jn. 15:1ff.; Rev. 21:2, 9; 22:17.

But though the Church is the Messianic Community, the fulfilment of Old Testament prophecy and the realization of the true Israel, it must be remembered that in one respect at least, the People of the New Covenant are radically different. Israel (despite the protests of the greatest of the post-Exilic prophets) remained an ethnic group, the seed of Abraham, and full membership of the nation belonged only to free-born male Jews. The Church knows no such restrictions: in Christ there is not only a unity, but a universality,[1] and the "seed of Abraham" becomes all the sons and daughters of Adam.

Although the word *ekklēsia* occurs only three times in St. Matthew,[2] and nowhere else in the Gospels, the community of Christians is spoken of as the *flock* or *little flock*,[3] while Jesus's self-designation as the *Son of Man* (who, in its source in Daniel 7, is the representative and embodiment of the people of God), clearly implies a community. The Epistles and Acts use the word freely, both in singular and plural. Sometimes the location is added—"the churches of Asia", "the church of the Thessalonians", and sometimes the church is said to be "the church of God",[4] or "of Christ",[5] but even where this is not stated, it is *implied* that the Church is God's. True, the Church can be the Church "of the saints",[6] but that does not make it man's, for the saints themselves are, by definition, those who belong to God.

As to symbolism, the figures used of the Christian community as alternatives to the use of *ekklēsia* itself are, perhaps, even more instructive. Body, Temple, Spiritual House, Royal Priesthood, Holy Nation[7] and the metaphors Vine and Bride mentioned above, all make it abundantly clear that the Church

[1] I Cor. 12:13; Gal. 3:28.
[2] Mt. 16:18 and twice in 18:17.
[3] Mt. 26:31; Lk. 12:32.
[4] Acts 20:28; I Tim. 3:5.
[5] Rom. 16:16; cf. I Thess. 2:14 for an even fuller designation.
[6] I Cor. 14:33.
[7] Eph. 1:22; 5:22f.; I Cor. 3:16f.; 2 Cor. 6:16; I Pet. 2:5, 9 etc.

depends upon Christ as its head (or foundation), and that, like Israel, it is peculiarly God's own possession. Some of the metaphors (e.g. Temple, Priesthood) strikingly indicate that, again like Israel, the Church is cast for a missionary rôle.

About the *organization* of the New Testament Church, we know relatively little, and we may guess that, in its infancy, the organization was rudimentary. At a very early stage, perhaps because of the expected speedy return of Christ, the members of the Jerusalem church sold their possessions, pooled the proceeds and began to live on a communistic basis.[1] When the system broke down, the other churches came to the rescue by making a collection for the Jerusalem Christians.[2] This incident shows that there was no *uniformity*: the other churches did not follow Jerusalem's lead. But there was *unity*: when there was a crisis in the one church, the others felt an obligation to come to its aid. There seems to have been an early attempt to impose the will of the Judaean church on the gentile missions (Acts 15), but the attempt, which might well have been disastrous, came to nothing. Paul seems to have discouraged marriage,[3] but only on the grounds that it was hardly worth while to change one's condition for the short time that remained before the *Parousia*, not because celibacy was considered more honourable than the married state. Celibacy was certainly never the general rule, even in the earliest times, and 1 Cor. 9:5 appears to be a protest against the idea that it should be. As hope of an early return of Christ waned, the Church no doubt felt the need of a more settled and permanent structure, but no uniform organization had emerged by the time the last of the New Testament documents were written; as at all times of rapid expansion, the Church of the Apostles was far too busy with the task of evangelization to bother about formal organization!

The little that we do know from the New Testament about worship, ministry, sacraments, will be referred to presently.

[1] Acts 4:32.   [2] 1 Cor. 16:1.   [3] 1 Cor. 7:8.

What is very evident is that from the earliest times, the Church was seen to be *one*; while there were local gatherings of Christians meeting in private houses,[1] and sometimes more than one in a city, all were part of an organic whole of which all believers were members, and to which converts naturally became attached.[2]

In more recent times, there has been debate about whether the Church is properly *visible* (i.e. the organizational Church—God's elect) or *invisible*. On the latter view, only God knows who are the members of the true Church; and members of the organizational Church may or may not be included in it (cf. Augustine's class of men elected only to membership of the Church, not to salvation). Conceivably, on this view, some outside the organizational Church may be within the true Church. While some sayings of Jesus appear to favour this view,[3] the New Testament, on the whole, assumes that the Church is a visible society whose members can be known, and that all who profess the Christian Faith will belong to it. Conversely, those who betray Christ and His Church are removed from the fellowship.[4] That fellowship is the fellowship of the Holy Spirit, the Spirit of God, or of Christ, and a fellowship that has not received the Spirit is defective.[5] Everything is done *in*, *by* or *through* the Spirit, and indeed, the Church sees itself as the sphere of the Spirit's activity—another indication that it is essentially a divine, not a human institution.

The Relation of Church and Kingdom

It is obvious to any reader of the New Testament that the two are related, but it is not immediately clear what the relationship is. In the Synoptic Gospels, Jesus constantly speaks of the Kingdom of God (or of Heaven) which His coming has

[1] Rom. 16:3–5. [2] Acts 2:47.
[3] Mk. 9:40; Mt. 7:21–23; Jn. 10:16. [4] Acts 1:15–26; 5:1–11.
[5] Acts 8:14–16; 19:1–6.

inaugurated[1] and to which believers belong, while in the Fourth Gospel, *life* has much the place that Kingdom has in the Synoptics; indeed, Mk. 9:43,45,47 shows that even in the Synoptics, *life* and *Kingdom* are practically synonymous. But *Church* and *Kingdom* are not synonymous: Lk. 12:32 states that the *little flock* is heir to the Kingdom, and in the Epistles and Acts, where Church is more prominent than Kingdom and may seem at a casual reading to have taken its place, closer study shows a Christian community that prays for the coming of Christ's rule in all its fullness,[2] and awaits it in faith. The overall New Testament picture, then, is that the Kingdom has come, and men may be born into it,[3] but it is not yet fully realized. Slowly and surely, the Kingdom will grow[4] until the time when "all the kingdoms of this world become the Kingdom of our God and of His Christ",[5] and the Church militant on earth strives to that end. The Church is not an end in itself; while it is *holy* (belonging exclusively to God), *catholic* (embracing the whole earth, and teaching the whole faith) and *apostolic* (having the same religious experience and evangelistic zeal as the Disciples), it is not eternal. We may speak of "the church triumphant in heaven" only in the sense that death has no finality for Christians, and therefore the faithful who have died are still part of the fellowship of believers (what the Apostles' Creed calls the *communion of saints*) which the grave cannot divide. That sense apart, the Church is a pilgrim Church, the earthly sphere of the Kingdom's present activity, and when the Kingdom is fully come, the Church's work will have been completed, and Church and Kingdom will then be synonymous.[6]

[1] Cf. Lk. 11:20.
[2] I Cor. 16:22; Rev. 22:20; cf. Mt. 6:10.
[3] Jn. 3:3, 5.
[4] Mk. 4:26ff.; 4:30ff.
[5] Rev. 11:15.
[6] Cf. Rev. 21:22.

2. Historical Development

As the success of Gentile missions made the Church increasingly catholic in the sense of embracing more and more of the known world, the need for ensuring that it remained Catholic in the other sense (that of proclaiming the whole authentic Gospel), became more urgent. With the delay of the *Parousia*, and the death of the first eye-witnesses of the Gospel events, it was clearly necessary to provide for the leadership of the Church in the second generation, and to have some reliable and authoritative written statements of Christian belief. Gradually, church organization evolved into an hierarchical system of bishops, presbyters[1] (or elders) and deacons claiming apostolic authority and claiming to be the custodians of the authentic Gospel tradition. Slowly, the Church became a tightly disciplined movement with formalized rites of initiation, established forms of worship, minimum standards of belief expressed in short credal statements, and with an accepted canon of scripture to which Christians could appeal for verification of their beliefs, and which could itself claim authority as the embodiment of the Faith. The Church claimed to be based on scripture, and scripture was authorized by the Church; the word of scripture and Church tradition supported and validated each other, and the two have remained the twin pillars of orthodoxy.

Minor and temporary schisms apart, it can be said that the Church was one and undivided until A.D. 1054 when the Eastern (Greek) Church severed its connections with the rest of Christendom. From then on, there were two parallel traditions, the Western (Catholic) and the Eastern (Orthodox), the one owning allegiance to Rome, the other to Constantinople, and both claiming apostolic authority. The two traditions continued side by side until the Reformation (sixteenth century) introduced a third factor. On the face of it, this third

[1] Gk. *presbüteroi.*

factor was the assertion of the primacy of scripture over tradition as the arbiter of faith and practice, and in particular, of the fundamental importance of the long-neglected Pauline doctrine of salvation by grace through faith,[1] but in fact, the Reformation was both more and less than that.

The upheaval that took place in the Church was vastly complex. The spirit of the Renaissance was at work throughout Europe, and everywhere the old order was being challenged, no less in science than in religion; Copernicus and Luther were contemporaries, and Galileo was born the year that Calvin died. For two centuries, the West was in a ferment from which practically nothing emerged unchanged. As men asserted the right of private judgment, so nations claimed the right of self-determination, and in some other countries, as in England, the break with Rome was both a demonstration of political independence, and a declaration of spiritual freedom. The first rumblings of revolt against a corrupt papacy had indeed been heard more than a century before Luther, and indicated clearly enough that the coming struggle would be political as well as religious. Wyclif in England (d. A.D. 1384) was saved from execution as a heretic only by the protection of John o' Gaunt, while the martyrdom of Huss in Bohemia (A.D. 1415) led to a long and bloody civil war. It was to be expected that the final break with Rome, when it did come, would have political and nationalist overtones or undertones.

In fact, the Reformation of the sixteenth century gave rise to a number of national, confessional Churches holding services mostly in the vernacular, and owning allegiance to the State instead of to the Chair of St. Peter. The several Protestant Churches were *confessional* in that they drew up confessions of faith,[2] not to replace ancient Catholic doctrine, but to

[1] The three great principles, *sola fide, sola gratia, sola scriptura*.

[2] E.g. *The Confession of Augsburg*, 1530 (Lutheran); *The Heidelberg Catechism*, 1563 (Reformed or Calvinist); *The Westminster Confession*, 1646–47, now used by English-speaking Presbyterian Communions.

indicate the way in which the traditional Faith ought rightly to be interpreted. All the Reformation Churches held to the ancient creeds and so had a claim to true catholicity of doctrine, but they maintained the right to freedom in matters of worship and church order. The twin streams of the Reformation, Lutheranism and Calvinism, gave rise in some regions to two Protestant Churches living and working independently, and subsequent disputes about baptism (believers' *versus* infant), church government (episcopal *versus* presbyterian) and election (Calvinism *versus* Arminianism) as well as arguments about how much state control of ecclesiastical functions could be tolerated, led to still further proliferation of church bodies. Within a couple of centuries the number of separate communions in the Christian West was considerable, but the international outlook of the great Church leaders, and their contacts with each other, preserved the essential unity of the Reformation and ensured that there was a form of churchmanship that could be recognized and identified as Protestant. Nevertheless, it could no longer reasonably be said (except by Roman Catholics, who recognized no Church but their own), that one Church embraced the West, let alone the world. It there was "one church", then (except on the Roman view) if must be the one invisible Church, the elect known only to God and scattered, no doubt, in all the several denominations. This has generally been the Protestant position, and most would, perhaps, echo the words of Luther: "The Church is found everywhere in the world where the Gospel and the Sacraments are found."

Ecumenism

Both Roman Catholic and Protestant attitudes have softened over the centuries, and engagement in worldwide missions and the need to combat the increasing secularization of society, have fostered understanding between the Churches and encouraged movements towards reunion. What is called ecumenism (or œcumenism—from Gk. *oikoumenē*—the inhabited world) is one of the most prominent features of the contemporary Church scene; Christians are conscious as never before of "the sinfulness of our divisions", and attempts to heal the breaches are constantly being made. What Christians are not agreed about is whether it is the *physical* separation of the Churches that is contrary to God's will, or only *spiritual* divisions due to our failure to work together in love and charity. Christians of all denominations generally claim that their Churches are led by the Spirit, and that they believe their practices to be in accord with the will of God *for them*. Where conscience is involved, compromises cannot be embraced simply to achieve a visible unity of the Church, and indeed it may be that all that God requires, and man may expect, is a Church visibly united in faith and work. Co-operation within the World Council of Churches, and between it and the Roman Communion, will no doubt grow apace, and further union schemes in various parts of the globe will come into operation, but it may be doubted if the Body of Christ will ever be physically one and undivided, and to require such an organic unity may be to press a metaphor too far.[1]

3. Constructive Statement

For the present, the Body of Christ is a divided Body comprising Roman Catholic, Orthodox and Protestant members, all recognizing Christ as unquestionably Head of the Body, all professing the essential doctrines of the Faith, and all able to point to the success of their missionary enterprises as

[1] For a sharp criticism of "mergers" and "organic unions" and a defence of denominationalism, see Ian Henderson, *Power without Glory* (1967). Henderson argues that the idea of a single organizational Church is inappropriate in the modern pluralist society, and that denominationalism, while not ideal, protects freedom, tolerance and healthy diversity in religion.

evidence of the Spirit's presence. What divides the Church are such doctrines as the *Immaculate Conception* (of Mary),[1] the *Assumption of Mary*,[2] the number of the sacraments, Papal Infallibility, Apostolic Succession; organizational matters like episcopacy, marriage of the clergy, establishment; moral issues—divorce, family planning, legalized abortion etc. The visible Church is not divided on the vital doctrines of the Faith, on those doctrines that are in any way necessary to salvation.

While the existence of separate denominations may not be in accord with the ideal will of God, the several communions may well have undertaken more missionary work in the last two or three centuries than a single, united Church would have done. On that there will obviously be differences of opinion. If, sometimes, denominational rivalry has been a dominant motive of evangelistic work, even that may not be totally damning:

> Some indeed preach Christ even of envy and strife; and some also of good will: . . . What then? only that, in every way, whether in pretence or in truth, Christ is proclaimed; and therein I rejoice, yea, and will rejoice. (Phil. 1:15, 18)

What is always damning is uncharity of outlook, and the censorious spirit that leads one Christian to condemn another.

Unfortunately, practical considerations involve us in passing judgment on others. Once we accept the necessity for, and the existence of, a visible Church, we have to define (if only roughly) its boundaries. Who are Christians and who are not?

---

[1] The doctrine, defined by Pius IX in 1854, that Mary was *herself* conceived without the stain of original guilt. The dogma has nothing whatever to do with the conception of *Jesus*—that is the doctrine of the *Virgin Birth*. The dogma is generally rejected by Protestants and modern Orthodox.

[2] Defined by Pius XII in 1950—at the end of her earthly life, Mary was taken up, body and soul into the glory of heaven. Accepted by Romans and Orthodox, rejected by Protestants.

In the absolute sense, of course, only God knows, but for our immediate purposes we generally exclude all those religious bodies that deny the divinity of Jesus Christ, and all whose tenets seem generally to be at variance with traditional Christian theology as contained in the Creeds. On the other hand, we generally include the Salvation Army and the Quakers, though they lack one of the recognized marks of the Church — the celebration of the sacraments. It is right that we restrict such judgments to the absolute minimum consistent with preserving the Faith against gross distortion.

To sum up, we conclude that the Church was founded by Jesus Christ, endowed with the Holy Spirit, and charged with the earthly work of the Kingdom but that, from the start, it was fallible and imperfect, and no doubt included some who were not part of the Church invisible. Its history has at every stage exhibited the same imperfection; the Church has been a frail earthen vessel, sometimes worldly, often lax, and always unworthy of its calling, but it has been the main sphere of the Spirit's activity among men, and the instrument for the spreading of the Gospel. If the members of the Church are not to be equated with the elect, nor the Church with the Kingdom, it is nevertheless true that the earthly, visible *ekklēsia* is the normal sphere of spiritual life and work of those who are being saved, and probably it is true that "outside the Church there is no salvation", though we must be careful not to draw the boundaries of the Church too rigidly. It is not for us lightly to unchurch any man who will sincerely affirm *Jesus is Lord!* Indeed, those words[1] may well have been the earliest Christian creed, but, in any case, it is personal faith and obedience that are the essence of Christian discipleship and the foundation, humanly speaking, on which the Church stands.[2]

[1] 1 Cor. 12:3.   [2] Mt. 16:17f.

8

THE MINISTRY

1. Biblical

After the Ascension, the leadership of·the Church naturally fell to the Twelve, the men who had originally been appointed by Jesus "that they might be with him, and that he might send them forth to preach",[1] and who had a continuing responsibility to spread the Gospel.[2] Matthias took the place vacated by Iscariot, and later Paul became the Apostle to the Gentiles; both had the indispensable qualification for the Apostolate—that they were first-hand witnesses of the Resurrection, and therefore able to preach it with authority.[3] These thirteen, with James the brother of Jesus who would have had a natural authority, became the recognized leaders of the Church. The rapid growth of the Christian community, and the problems to which it gave rise, led to the appointment of "the seven",[4] who are generally supposed to have been deacons. Although the seven were appointed by the Apostles to distribute alms, they had to be "men full of the spirit" and two of them at least (Stephen and Philip) immediately engaged in preaching. The organization of the infant Church, such as

[1] Mk. 3:14.
[2] Acts 1:8; cf. Mt. 28:19f.
[3] Acts 1:21f.; 1 Cor. 15:8f.
[4] Acts 6:1–6.

it was, was directed towards the proclamation of the Gospel, and it is significant that in Paul's two lists of the gifts of the Spirit, apostles, prophets and teachers have pride of place.[1] The relationship of apostles and prophets is not at all clear, and the *Didache*, a Jewish-Christian work written, most probably, soon after A.D. 100, treats them as if they were the same.[2] Perhaps they were; at any rate, little is heard of the prophets after the close of the Apostolic period.

As we have seen, the Twelve appointed the deacons, and soon we find mention of bishops (*episcopoi*) and elders (*presbüteroi*). Probably these also were one order: in Acts 20:28, the Ephesian elders are called "bishops", and the church at Philippi seems to have had a number of bishops and deacons, but there is no mention of elders.[3] There appears to have been a two-fold local ministry of presbyter-bishops and deacons, and we know very little about the functions of either. Evidently elders (or bishops) were appointed in some local churches,[4] and from the desirable qualifications stated in 1 Timothy 3:1-7, they were apparently intended to teach and superintend the church and to represent it in its dealings with the outside world.

The New Testament shows us a Church with two quite different ministries existing together, and no doubt overlapping: (i) a charismatic ministry of those with gifts of prophecy, healing, "speaking with tongues" (*glossolalia*), and interpretation of tongues etc. Perhaps these would be itinerant or at least, not attached to any particular church or town. They would not be formally appointed, and such authority as they enjoyed would rest upon the powers they were seen to possess: (ii) a local ministry of presbyter-bishops and deacons appointed by the Apostles or elected by the con-

[1] 1 Cor. 12:28; Eph. 4:11.
[2] *Didache*, XI.
[3] Phil. 1:1.
[4] Acts 14:23; Tit. 1:5–7.

gregation on the basis of their general fitness, and charged with pastoral oversight and instruction of converts in the community. Certainly the charismatic ministries were the more important in the early period; what mattered about Philip was not that he had been appointed deacon, but that he was an evangelist with four daughters who prophesied,[1] and the rapid rise of Apollos[2] indicates again that it was obvious Spirit-endowment, not formal status, that counted.

It is useless to look to the New Testament for support for any one form of ecclesiastical organization; we cannot say that church government in the earliest period was episcopalian, or that it was presbyterian and probably we must conclude that there was no fixed pattern. One thing that can be said quite definitely, however, is that the Church had no priests, or rather, that all believers were priests, and Christ the High Priest from whom they derived their priesthood.[3] There is no mention whatever of a priestly ministry reserved to a particular group, and consequently there is no division of the Church into priesthood and laity. That division came later and has no warrant in the New Testament.

Christian ministry, of course, is not simply a matter of religious personnel, but of acts of fellowship, worship, discipline etc. and here again our knowledge is scanty. From the beginning, Christians met for teaching, for "the breaking of bread" (the Eucharist and/or Agapē) and for prayers, the latter sometimes, at first, in the Jerusalem Temple.[4] The first believers interpreted fellowship as a true sharing of God's gifts; necessitous widows were looked after,[5] and as we saw earlier, the churches of Corinth and Galatia made collections for the relief of Christians in Jerusalem.[6] In its worship, the Church used "hymns and spiritual songs",[7] probably the Psalter and such Christian hymns as *Magnificat, Benedictus, Gloria in*

[1] Acts 21:8f.   [2] Acts 18:24ff.   [3] 1 Pet. 2:5, 9; Rev. 1:6.
   [4] Acts 2:42, 46; 1 Cor. 11:20ff.   [5] Acts 6:1ff.
   [6] 1 Cor 16:1ff.   [7] Eph. 5:19.

Excelsis and *Nunc Dimittis*, along with others of which Philippians 2:6-11, 1 Timothy 3:16 and 1 Corinthians 13 may be examples. Worship certainly included from time to time, spontaneous prophecy and ecstatic utterance,[1] though the latter was not much favoured by St. Paul. Healing and exorcism were practised, and indeed had been commanded by Jesus Himself,[2] while open confession of sins seems to have been the rule.[3] In general, it may be said that the Church's worship was rich, spontaneous and informal, and very much a free expression of the experience of the Holy Spirit.

2. Historical Development

In the first three centuries, when persecution was sporadic and often regional, the local leaders would obviously play a vital rôle in encouraging the faithful, and by their personal courage under torture, many bishops aroused admiration among Christians and non-Christians alike. With the death of the first disciples, and the gradual decline of the charismatic ministries as the spiritual impetus of Pentecost waned, the presbyter-bishops assumed more authority, and by about A.D. 112, Ignatius of Antioch is writing: "Let no man perform anything pertaining to the Church without the bishop", and "It is not permitted either to baptise or hold a love-feast apart from the bishop".[4] What is not clear is whether Ignatius is stating what had already become established practice, or pleading for a greater measure of authority for the bishops than in fact they enjoyed. In A.D. 180, Irenaeus, Bishop of Lyons, speaks of the succession of bishops in Rome, from the Apostles, Peter and Paul to his own day,

[1] Acts 19:6; 1 Cor. 14:1-25.
[2] Mt. 10:8; Acts 10:36ff.; Jas. 5:14f.
[3] Jas. 5:16.
[4] *Epistle to the Smyrnians*, VIII (Bettenson, *Documents of the Christian Church*, p. 90).

and certainly the Roman See came to have a special place and authority. By A.D. 451, the Council of Chalcedon could say: "Peter has spoken through Leo (Bishop of Rome at the time). . . . Anathema to him who believes otherwise." Slowly, the Bishop of Rome had become the Pope.

With the end of persecution, and the settlement under Constantine,[1] Christianity became the established Faith of the Empire, and bishops became increasingly important in civil as well as ecclesiastical affairs. Eventually the Church became rich and the bishops powerful; in the Middle Ages they, and the heads of monasteries, were great land owners, and as their power grew, so the power of the Papacy increased until it had the whole of the West in its grip.

At the Reformation, despite the breach with Rome, episcopacy continued in some Protestant churches (some Lutheran, and later the Moravian, for example) but these bishops had not the immense political and economic prestige of the Medieval prelates. The Church of England continued to have bishops, still with some princely functions and living in considerable state, but by the beginning of the present century, apart from the most senior bishops' membership of the House of Lords, episcopal authority had become largely confined to the Church.

Some Protestant churches, however, rejected episcopacy in favour of presbyterian government (rule by elders or presbyters) e.g. the Reformed or Calvinist churches, of which the Church of Scotland is a British example. Later communions such as the Baptists and Independents (Congregationalists) represent a third form of church organization in which authority resides mainly in the local congregation, while British Methodism has a modified form of presbyterian government.

---

[1] *Edict of Toleration* (A.D. 311); *Edict of Milan* (A.D. 313) (Bettenson, 21f.).

As already hinted, there has been, from very early times,[1] a doctrine of Apostolic Succession—an unbroken line of bishops traceable to Peter and Paul, transmitting apostolic authority from one to another, and thus preserving the true Catholic tradition.[2] There is no agreement at present whether Lutheran and Anglican bishops (for instance) are properly in that succession, and in any case, the historical evidence for an unbroken succession is more than dubious. If there were such a succession, it is not clear what apostolic authority it could transmit; certainly not the essential authority that belonged to them as eye-witnesses of the Gospel events! Protestants generally reject Apostolic Succession, or at least, give it a very subordinate place, regarding it as a picturesque symbol of the continuity of the Church.[3] Sometimes they speak of a *spiritual succession*, passing through such great figures as Augustine, Luther and Wesley,[4] but they would strongly deny that the validity of orders and Church rites in any way derives from a mechanical succession, for the Spirit cannot be bound in that sort of way.

3. Constructive Statement

The variety and richness of ministry in the Early Church is only now being regained; the present missionary era, comparable with that of the first centuries, has called for a greater flexibility in men and techniques, while modern insights into the nature of illness have awakened a fresh interest in spiritual healing. The confusion of modern society has alerted

[1] E.g. Hegesippus, *c.* A.D. 175.

[2] Cf. Irenaeus, *Adv. Haeres.* III, iii, 1–2.

[3] For this symbolic view of the *succession*, I am indebted to Principal A. R. George.

[4] Luther read and was influenced by Augustine, and Wesley stood in the same relationship to Luther.

the Church to the need to fulfil a truly prophetic function. At the same time, most Christians are now willing to admit that the formal structure of the Church throughout the centuries has preserved the Faith as we know it. Despite the fact that there has been no shortage of heretical bishops (e.g. Apollinarius, Nestorius), despite worldliness and laxity among prelates, especially in the Medieval period, the episcopal system that was universal until the Reformation undoubtedly played a great part in safeguarding the Church against grave error. Perhaps presbyterian government, had it then obtained, would have done as much, but that we shall never know.

At the present time, bishops of all communions are more recognizably the *servants* of the Church, and more ready to consult the laity on important matters, so that some of the former objections to a "proud prelacy" are no longer valid. Indeed, in certain modern united churches operating on an episcopal basis (e.g. South India), bishops are seen again in their New Testament rôle as shepherds and pastors, a form of *episcopē* that can commend itself even to convinced presbyterians. Perhaps, as the Churches come together, there is now a greater awareness that no current system of church government can claim exclusive New Testament authority, and a growing realization that the Church's ministry is a many-coloured thing in which all the people (*laos*) of God share. Perhaps we are becoming conscious that the New Testament words for ministry all imply service rather than status, and that it is service, in all its forms, that is the essence of ministry, from which it follows that in every age, that ministry will be best and most fitting that best serves the ends of the Kingdom in its day.

9

THE SACRAMENTS

The Prayer Book definition of *sacrament*—"an outward and visible sign of an inward and spiritual grace"—recalls the origin of the word: *sacramentum* was the Roman soldier's oath of allegiance, the outward and visible sign of his loyalty to the Emperor. Of these outward signs of inward grace, Roman and Eastern Churches recognize seven—baptism, confirmation, the Lord's Supper, penance, ordination, marriage and extreme unction (the "last rites"[1]), while Anglicans and most Protestants acknowledge two only, baptism and the Lord's Supper. These, alone of the seven, are the sacraments instituted by Jesus Christ, and the present discussion will be confined to them.

A. BAPTISM [1. Biblical]

There is no mention of baptism in the Old Testament, but the success of the Baptist's ministry[2] suggests that a

---

[1] This term may include both *anointing* ("*extreme unction*") and the *viaticum*—administration of the Eucharist as a preparation for the journey of death.

[2] Mk. 1:5.

similar water rite was known in contemporary Judaism, and, indeed, the *Mishnah*[1] says that Jews baptized proselytes (Gentile converts); whether the ceremony was a ritual cleansing, or an initiation, is disputed. John's "baptism of repentance unto remission of sins" was initiation into the Messianic age, and a means of fleeing "the wrath to come",[2] but he saw it as incomplete, a preparation for the baptism that would be "with the Holy Spirit" (Mk. 1:8) or "with the Holy Spirit and with Fire" (Mt. 3:11). In fact, contrary to John's expectation, Jesus seems not to have baptized,[3] and His Disciples may have done so only after the Resurrection had completed the work of redemption. Thereafter, baptism was universal as the sole means of admission to the Church,[4] and was invariably accompanied by the gift of the Holy Spirit, which sometimes preceded immersion[5] and sometimes followed, being imparted by the laying on of hands.[6] Performance of the rite was not confined to apostles,[7] and even when an apostle baptized the first converts in a town, local church officials seem to have been left to baptize the others.[8] There is no mention of infant baptism, though we hear of the baptism of whole households,[9] and these may have included children; certainly, baptism of infants is nowhere forbidden, if it is nowhere enjoined.

The symbolism of baptism is particularly rich. Obviously, water symbolizes cleansing, washing away sin;[10] less obviously, it symbolizes death—the water burial of the old

---

[1] A compilation of rabbinic teaching made *c.* A.D. 200.
[2] Lk. 3:7ff.; Mk. 1:4.
[3] Jn. 4:2.
[4] Acts 2:38–41; 9:18; 19:5 etc.
[5] Acts 10:44–48; 11:15–18.
[6] Acts 8:14ff.
[7] Acts 8:38; 9:18.
[8] 1 Cor. 1:14ff.
[9] Acts 16:15; 1 Cor. 1:16.
[10] Acts 22:16; 1 Cor. 6:11; Eph. 5:26; Tit. 3:5.

nature. Significantly, Jesus referred to His death as a baptism,[1] and Paul sees Christian baptism as an incorporation into the death and Resurrection of Jesus.[2] In other words, the baptized Christian is a new creation, so that baptism can be described as rebirth or *regeneration* (cf. Jn. 3:5), the beginning of a new life, to be followed by a process of growth in grace that we usually call *sanctification*.

While the origin of baptism is not to be sought in the Old Testament, Paul sees a *type* of baptism in the Israelites' Exodus experience, and can say that they "were baptized . . . in the cloud and in the sea" (1 Cor. 10:2). In both cases the passing through water is the gaining of freedom; in one case, escape from the slavery of Egypt, in the other, freedom from the bondage of sin.

2. Historical Development

Though in the first two centuries there were variations from place to place, the rite seems always to have included confession of faith, immersion[3] (though not necessarily *sub*mersion) in the Triune name, and generally, imposition of hands or confirmation. Variable local additions included fasting, vigil, renunciation of the Devil and/or exorcism, and anointing with oil (*chrism*); sometimes sponsors also were required. Through baptism, the candidate (generally called a *catechumen* while preparing for the sacrament) received forgiveness of sins, regeneration and the gift of the Holy Spirit. From the third century onwards, infant (or *paedo-*) baptism became increasingly common, especially where belief in Original Sin and guilt was strong, and gradually it became

[1] Lk. 12:50.

[2] Rom. 6:3f.; Col. 2:12.

[3] Except, presumably, when the rite took place in prison or on a deathbed, when *Affusion* (pouring on) or sprinkling of water would be used.

85

the general rule. At first, infants (like adults) received baptism and confirmation in the one rite, but later, in the West, the two became separated by a period of years, as they are in the modern Church. As infant baptism became common, the presence of sponsors, whose faith was given vicariously for the child, was increasingly stressed, and because of the high mortality rate of the very young, baptism carried out by a layman (even a heretic!) was often considered valid, especially if performed in emergency. Though there was no explicit New Testament warrant, infant baptism could be defended by appeal to such texts as Lk. 18:16f. and 1 Cor. 7:14, and on the general grounds that, in the Old Testament, children were within the covenant, and the New Covenant could hardly be less generous.

After the Reformation, both Lutheran and Reformed churches continued infant baptism, though insisting that it was *faith*, not the water of baptism, that was effective, the faith being either that of the sponsors and the congregation, or anticipatory of the personal faith the infant would later profess at confirmation. Anabaptists and Baptists insisted on believers' baptism, as do some other Protestant churches, but Anglicans, Presbyterians and Methodists have always practised the infant rite. Modern Roman Catholics also practise paedo-baptism, and still include exorcism in the sacrament. Protestants generally do not include it, though they may require the renunciation of the Devil and all his works (by the sponsors on behalf of the child)[1], or include prayers for the child's victory over the powers of evil.[2] Where believers' baptism is the rule, there is often a service of *dedication* for infants, as in some Baptist churches.

---

[1] So the Anglican *Book of Common Prayer*.
[2] E.g. the Methodist rite, *Book of Offices* (1936).

3. Constructive Statement

While some early practices were soon abandoned,[1] the sacrament in believers' or infant form has been all but universal throughout the Christian era. Some modern scholars find New Testament authority for paedo-baptism (O. Cullmann, J. Jeremias for instance), while others (like G. R. Beasley-Murray) deny it. Whatever the truth may be, it can be said that believers' baptism rightly stresses the prime importance of faith, while infant baptism, is a useful reminder that God's grace is always prior to man's response. Sometimes it is disputed whether the gift of the Holy Spirit is received at baptism (so D. Stone, G. W. H. Lampe), or at confirmation (Bishop Kirk, L. S. Thornton, G. Dix), but as A. Richardson has said, this dilemma arises only from the separation in time of what were originally parts of the one sacrament.

Infant baptism no doubt arose partly from the felt need for an infancy rite comparable with circumcision in Judaism,[2] and partly from the rapid expansion of Christendom, when mass conversion of the heathen called for a distinguishing mark for their children, but some of those who practise it (the majority of Christians), recognize that the infant baptized is less completely a member of the Church than the full-grown believer. In any case, as the Christian life is always a process of growth in grace, it is never possible to say at what point we become truly Christian, and to admit a young child to the Church is only to imitate what God does for us

[1] E.g. "Baptism for the dead" (1 Cor. 15:29), a vicarious baptism undergone by believers, apparently to obtain the benefits of salvation for dead, unbaptized relatives; also the practice of deferring baptism to the last days of life to avoid the possibility of post-baptismal sin, often thought to be unforgivable.

[2] Cf. Col. 2:11f. where circumcision and baptism are mentioned together.

all in "justifying the ungodly"—when He sees us not as we are but as what, by His grace, we shall become.

B. THE LORD'S SUPPER[1] [I. Biblical]

The earliest account of the institution of the sacrament is in 1 Corinthians 11:23–25, which agrees quite closely with the Synoptic record.[2] The Fourth Gospel, which devotes no less than five chapters (13 to 17) to the events in the upper room, does not mention the taking of bread and wine, though in an earlier passage, the words of institution are clearly in mind:

> Except ye eat the flesh of the Son of Man and drink his blood, ye have not life in yourselves. He that eateth my flesh and drinketh my blood hath eternal life; and I will raise him up at the last day. For my flesh is meat indeed, and my blood is drink indeed. He that eateth my flesh and drinketh my blood abideth in me, and I in him. (Jn. 6:53–56)

According to the Synoptics, the meal in the upper room was the Passover, but St. John[3] says it took place *before the Passover*, and his dating of the supper and subsequent events may well be right. In any case apparently, a full meal was eaten, with the blessing of bread at the beginning, in characteristic Jewish fashion, and the blessing of the cup at the end. Both Paul and Luke have the command *this do in remembrance* (*anamnēsis*) *of me*, but the one connects the words with the bread (Lk. 22:19), the other with both bread and wine (1 Cor. 11:24f.). The Synoptics and Paul all regard the wine as *the blood (cup) of the*

---

[1] Also called the *Eucharist* ("thanksgiving"—from *eucharistēsas*, Lk. 22:19), and the *Mass* (from the closing words of the Latin service: *ite missa est*—"go [the congregation] is dismissed"). *Holy Communion* is another name for the sacrament, though it is sometimes restricted to that part of the Eucharist or Mass in which priest and people take the elements.

[2] Mk. 14:22–24; Mt. 26:26–28; Lk. 22:19f.

[3] Jn. 13:1.

New Covenant and connect the inauguration of the Covenant with Jesus's impending death. In Matthew, Mark and Luke, the institution anticipates the Messianic feast in the Kingdom —*Until that day when I drink it new with you in my Father's kingdom*[1] while Paul has *For as often as ye eat this bread, and drink the cup, ye proclaim the Lord's death till he come*[2]—so that there is a definite eschatological element in all four accounts.

2. Historical Development

The "breaking of bread" was, from the first, a central feature of the Church's fellowship,[3] and was apparently a full meal. Later, what we call The Lord's Supper (bread and wine only) became detached from the rest of the meal, which was then observed as the *Agapē*, or Love Feast—a rite that fell into disuse about the seventh century, to be revived by the Moravians, the early Methodists and, in most recent times, by the current Liturgical Movement who have it, sometimes, as a parish breakfast following the Eucharist.

From post-Apostolic times, the sacrament seems to have been restricted to the baptized,[4] and a preparation by fasting and confession was often required. The importance of the Eucharist in the early Church cannot be exaggerated, and references to it in the Fathers are correspondingly numerous. Ignatius[5] calls it "the medicine of immortality which is the antidote against death, and gives eternal life in Jesus Christ". Similarly, Irenaeus[6] teaches:

> For as the bread of the earth, receiving the invocation of God, is no longer common bread but Eucharist, consisting of two things, an earthly and a heavenly; so also our bodies, partaking of the Eucharist, are no longer corruptible, having the hope of eternal resurrection.[7]

[1] Mt. 26:29.   [2] I Cor. 11:26.   [3] Acts 2:42,46; I Cor. 10:16; 11:26f.
[4] *Didache*, IX.   [5] *Ad Eph.* xx:2.   [6] *Adv. Haeres.* IV, xviii, 4–6.
[7] The translation is from Bettenson, p. 106.

Cyprian, Bishop of Carthage, A.D. 248–258, is the first to speak of the Eucharist as a complete sacrifice offered by the priest in imitation of what Christ did on the Cross.[1] What began in the upper room as a solemn Jewish meal, took on something of the form of a Temple sacrifice; increasingly the elements were actually *identified* with the body and blood of Christ, and the notes of thanksgiving, fellowship and commemoration became muted.

Medieval Schoolmen debated the way in which bread and wine were transformed into the body and blood, and as early as the twelfth century, Peter Lombard teaches that, as a result of consecration, the elements are changed into the substance of the body and blood, all that then remains of the bread and wine being their physical properties. This is the doctrine of *transubstantiation* which, by a decree of the Lateran Council (A.D. 1215), became orthodox Catholic teaching.[2]

The Reformation produced three different forms of Eucharistic theory:

(*1*) *Luther* teaches that the body of Christ is everywhere present in every meal, but it is uniquely present in the Eucharist. The elements are not transubstantiated[3] into the body and blood, but the real presence of Christ is *in*,

[1] Ep. lxiii, 14.

[2] In the twelfth century, the practice began of withdrawing the cup from the laity, and Aquinas justified this by teaching that *the whole Christ* was present in both species. The Council of Constance (A.D. 1415) made communion in one kind (bread only) compulsory. Nowadays, RC laity do receive the cup on a variety of special ocasions.

[3] Transubstantiation had led to a semi-magical view of the Eucharist with more and more emphasis on the supposed automatic effect of what was said and done, and less and less on what was *believed*, to the point of a popular reliance on the efficacy of the sacrament, whatever the spiritual state of the recipient. Common superstition, indeed, sometimes spoke of the priest, consecrating the elements, as "making God"(!), though official Catholicism never intended anything of the sort.

with and under the bread and wine. This doctrine is often called *consubstantiation*.

(2) *Zwingli*, a German-Swiss Reformer (1484–1531), denied that the Mass could be a repetition of the sacrifice of the Cross, and regarded the Supper as a *memorial* of that sacrifice. The bread and wine are symbols, and in the sacrament Christ is truly our food, but He is *received by faith*, not by mouth. The Eucharist is a communion, the pledge of our united allegiance to Christ. Zwingli therefore took the words of institution, "this *is* my body (blood)" to mean "this *signifies . . .*"

(3) *Calvin* denied both transubstantiation and consubstantiation, and taught that Christ is present *dynamically* in the bread and wine; in the elements, He is present *in power* to strengthen our living union with Him.

3. Constructive Statement

Deeper insights into the meaning of sacrifice, and the significance of the common meal—gained by the study of primitive religion, and the realization that in offering bread and wine, we offer not only God's gifts but man's labour—have led modern churchmen to look at the sacrament in a fresh light. Roman Catholics and High Anglicans continue to speak of Mass, sacrifice, altar and priest, while Protestants think in terms of thanksgiving, memorial, table and minister, and there is still wide divergence of opinion about the mode of Christ's presence in the meal (in the elements, or in the believer); but the differences are less marked than formerly. Catholics now emphasize the "once-for-allness" of the sacrifice of the Cross, instead of regarding the Mass as repeating or supplementing what Christ has done, while Protestants make more of the *real presence* than once they did. The gap is narrowing, and we may expect the present intensive interest in sacramental theology to bring about an even closer *rapprochement*, and to rediscover the varied significance of the rite as at once an act of fellowship, a memorial of the Passion, a sacrifice of praise and thanksgiving, and above all, a token and symbol of our union in the body of which Christ is the Head.

PART FOUR

THE DOCTRINE OF THE LAST THINGS
(ESCHATOLOGY)

IO

KINGDOM OF GOD, PAROUSIA, JUDGMENT, FUTURE LIFE

1. Biblical

In this final section, an attempt will be made to discover what Christianity has to say about the "one far-off divine event to which the whole creation moves"[1]—the end of the world-process which had its beginning at Creation and which, because it is not eternal, must sometime have a conclusion. The consummation of God's plan of redemption is conceived in various ways by biblical writers, and we shall have to summarize what they have to say under each main head; but because the several elements in Christian eschatology are so closely intertwined, our closing discussion will deal with the subject as a whole.

Kingdom of God

The popular response to the Baptist's announcement that the Kingdom of God was at hand, and to his demand for repentance,[2] shows that the establishment of the kingly rule of God was commonly expected, and that it was believed to

[1] Tennyson, *In Memoriam*, st. xxxvi.
[2] Mt. 3:2.

imply a moral and spiritual reckoning: the Kingdom to be inaugurated would be a righteous Kingdom, and its inception would involve the overthrow of evil and the punishment of the wicked. Originally, Hebrew religion had regarded reward and punishment as automatic: God meted out suffering to the wicked and prosperity to the righteous, so that men got their deserts in life. That was the orthodox view represented by the three friends of Job,[1] and it proved, of course, untenable. Experience taught that the righteous often go unrewarded in this life, while the wicked go scot-free. To reconcile this state of affairs with belief in a righteous God, it was necessary to suppose that, at some *future* time, Yahweh would call men and nations to account, and give them their deserts.

Hebrew prophecy had generally seen God achieving His ends indirectly by human agencies[2]—which is why the Prophets had been so actively involved in political affairs both within Israel and outside[3]—but as repeated disappointments led to a despair that things would ever be set to rights by anything man could do, there was a growing conviction that nothing short of a catastrophic intervention by Yahweh Himself would establish the reign of righteousness and peace. More and more the seers began to look for the Day of the Lord, when judgment would be pronounced on Israel and the Nations, and the doom of the wicked would be sealed. So we have a succession of Prophets giving increasingly lurid descriptions of that Day, and of the awesome circumstances that would surround it,[4] and these passages represent the transition from prophecy to a new form of literature,

[1] Job 4:7-9; cf. Ps. 37 etc.

[2] Cf. Ex. 3; Jud. 4:1-3; Isa. 10:5; 45:1.

[3] Cf. the careers of Elijah and Jeremiah, who were especially involved in external politics.

[4] Amos 5:18; Zeph. 1:14ff.; Isa. 13:10ff.; Joel 2:30ff.; 3:2, 4, 12.

apocalyptic,[1] which was eventually to replace it almost completely. By the time the Baptist appeared, Israel's hope rested upon the belief that God would intervene personally to vindicate the righteous and chastize the ungodly. Judaism remained a "this-worldly" religion; vindication was not looked for in some future life beyond, but on this terrestrial plane, an attitude reflected in the angelic message of Luke 2:14, and the petitions of the Lord's Prayer, "Thy kingdom come. Thy will be done, as in heaven, so on earth".

This earthly kingdom would be set up by the Messiah,[2] a prince of Davidic descent, and would be the golden age in which Israel's former glory, enjoyed all too briefly in David's reign, would be restored, never to be lost again. What Messianic prophecy had to say about judgment on Israel's sin was largely forgotten in the eager expectation that the nation, so long down-trodden by powerful neighbours, would at last have her rightful place. If John the Baptist saw the advent of Messiah as the coming of judgment on the wicked in Israel, most Jews saw it as the prospect of national aggrandizement.

Two other strands of Old Testament expectation, however, left little room for patriotic and nationalistic pretensions. One of these was the *Suffering Servant* of Isaiah,[3] the personification of the ideal Israel, purified and chastened by the Exile and destined to be God's missionary agent among the

---

[1] From Gk. *apocalüpsis*—uncovering or revelation. Apocalyptic works multiplied between 165 B.C. and A.D. 100, some of the more important being *Enoch, Testament of the Twelve Patriarchs, Assumption of Moses, Ascension of Isaiah*. Apocalyptic writings are generally pseudonymous, written in the name of some great figure of the past, and are highly imaginative and rich in symbolism. There are apocalyptic elements in Ezek. 1; Dan. 2, 7, 8; NT examples are in Mk. 13 and parallels, and of course, in Revelation, otherwise called *The Apocalypse*.

[2] Heb. for *anointed*: the Gk. equivalent is *Christos* = Christ.

[3] The *Servant Songs*—Isa. 42:1–4; 49:1–6; 50:4–9; 52:13–53:12.

Nations—a rôle that would call for suffering and sacrifice. According to John 1:36, the Baptist seems to have connected Jesus with the Suffering Servant, and Jesus certainly saw His destiny in those terms.[1] The other was the *Son of Man* motif, first occurring in Daniel 7 and again, not as the designation of an individual, but as the embodiment of Israel—*the people of the saints of the Most High*. Son of Man is an apocalyptic figure subsequently elaborated in the Book of Enoch,[2] and in line with apocalyptic thought, the emphasis is on the element of direct divine intervention. The Son of Man is from above: judgment is established and the Kingdom set up by the exercise of Yahweh's sovereign power. Jesus certainly favoured this view of the coming of the Kingdom, and generally spoke of Himself as Son of Man rather than Messiah.

In the Synoptic Gospels, Kingdom is a dominant theme, and its nature and development are the subject of many of the parables. On the one hand, the Kingdom is growing unobserved from small beginnings to vast proportions;[3] it is the ferment working quietly in society and destined ultimately to transform it.[4] On the other hand, the Kingdom is a present reality to which Jesus's exorcisms bear witness: *If I by the finger of God cast out devils, then is the Kingdom of God come upon you.* (Lk. 11:20)

The presence of the Kingdom represents a challenge, demands a response of repentance and faith,[5] and calls for self-denial and sacrifice on the part of the would-be entrant;[6] but as the Kingdom is a pearl of great price, a hidden treasure, no sacrifice is too great to gain it.[7]

---

[1] Mt. 16:21ff.; Mk. 10:45; cf. Acts 3:18; Phil. 2:7f.

[2] Enoch 48:1-10.

[3] "The Seed Growing Secretly" (Mk. 4:26f.); "The Mustard Seed" (Mt. 13:31f.).

[4] Mt. 13:33.

[5] Mk. 1:15, etc.

[6] Mk. 9:43-47; Lk. 9:57-62.

[7] Mt. 13:44-46.

The Fourth Gospel has relatively little to say about the Kingdom,[1] but has a great deal to say about *life*, and it is evident that the two are practically the same, as Mark 9:43; 45:47 shows they can be, even in the Synoptics. All four Gospels insist that entry into the new life of the Kingdom is conditional on faith in Jesus Christ, and all contain the same apparent contradiction between the Kingdom as already set up, and as still to be established in the future. The contradiction is more apparent than real, for as the Kingdom is the *reign*[2] of God, it will always be more or less complete in any place according to the response it has evoked; but however few they are, in any place or age who have responded in faith and obedience, the reign of God is a *fact*, and a fact that will be increasingly obvious as the Kingdom grows towards its consummation.

Parousia and Judgment

The consummation of the Kingdom is to be looked for at the *coming* or *coming again* of Christ, the Greek word for which is *Parousia*,[3] and the event is associated with judgment and the end of the world-order.

[1] But cf. Jn. 3, where the stress is on entrance to the Kingdom by rebirth.

[2] Reign as opposed to a territorial realm.

[3] The word may mean either *presence* or *coming*; it is twice used of Paul's presence (2 Cor. 10.10, Phil. 2.12), and thrice of the arrival of the Apostle or his helpers (1 Cor. 16:17; 2 Cor. 7:6; Phil 1:26). Of almost a score of cases in which *parousia* is used in the technical sense of the Second Advent, one (1 Cor. 15:23) speaks of the order of the resurrection, four of spiritual preparedness for the Coming (Mt. 24:37, 39; Jas. 5:7f.; 1 Jn. 2:28), while eight (Mt. 24:27; 1 Thess. 4:15; 2 Thess. 2:1, 8, 9; 2 Pet. 3:4, 12) contain obvious apocalyptic elements —lightning, the appearance of lawlessness in the Temple, the dissolution of the heavens, etc. One text (2 Pet. 1:16) refers to incidents in Jesus's ministry—baptism and transfiguration. *Parousia* is not the only word for the Second Advent: in 1 Cor. 1:7, the noun is *apocalüpsis* = "revealing", a clear indication that it is not a natural historical advent,

The Gospels. As we saw earlier, the Old Testament looked forward to the establishment of God's rule of peace and righteousness, and prophecy abounded in warnings about the terrors of God's wrath against wickedness that would then be experienced and, on the other hand, with descriptions of the idyllic conditions that Israel would enjoy when the reign of God had come in.[1] Both the prophetic announcements of the coming of Messiah, and apocalyptic expectation of the descent of the heavenly Son of Man were very much in men's minds at the dawn of the Christian era, and the Baptist's mission was a preparation for the imminent fulfilment of the nation's hope: the Day of the Lord was at hand, and redemptive history had reached its climax. New Testament writers all see the Incarnation as the realization of what the prophets taught and hoped for:[2] Christ has come, but the final judgment proves to be still in the future. The Baptist had graphically described the impending sorting out of wheat and chaff, and when this did not happen at the beginning of Jesus's ministry, doubts arose in his mind, and prompted the question, "Art thou he that should come, or look we for another?"[3] Jesus's reply was to point to His healing and preaching ministry as signs of the dawning of the Messianic Age, to acknowledge John as the forerunner, and to warn His unresponsive hearers of the fate awaiting them on the Day of Judgment.[4]

Jesus clearly associates judgment with His own return:

> For the Son of Man shall come in the glory of his Father with his angels; and then shall he render unto every man according to his deeds. (Mt. 16:27)

---

while in some relevant parables, the Coming is expressed by the verb *erchesthai*, "to come" (Lk. 12:45; 19:23).

[1] Isa. 9:6f.; 11:6ff., etc.

[2] Mt. 13:17; Lk. 4:18–21; Acts 13:25–32, etc.

[3] Mt. 11:3.

[4] Mt. 11:7–24.

Then shall they see the Son of Man coming in clouds with great power and glory. And then shall he send forth the angels, and shall gather together his elect from the four winds, from the uttermost part of the earth to the uttermost part of heaven. (Mk. 13:26f.)

The first of these passages, at least, speaks of the Coming as within the lifetime of the hearers. On the other hand, there is the warning that even Jesus and the angels do not know when the day will be[1]—hence the need for watchfulness and preparedness enjoined by the parables of "The Householder", "The Faithful Servant", and "The Ten Virgins".[2] In the meantime, pending the Day of Judgment, good and evil will coexist in the world, like weeds in a field of corn.[3] The Judgment will surely come, however, and we note that where Jesus speaks of it, He usually refers to Himself as the Son of Man—an indication that these sayings belong to the apocalyptic strand in the Gospels.

In a sense, of course, judgment has begun already:

He that believeth on him is not judged; he that believeth not hath been judged already, because he hath not believed on the name of the only begotten Son of God. (Jn. 3:18)

Such sayings as this, in their context, indicate that men are judged according to their faith (or lack of it)[4] and therefore, if

[1] Mk. 13:32–37. This apocalyptic chapter, and its parallels in Mt. 24 and Lk. 21, appear to have a double reference; to the siege of Jerusalem, which will come within a generation, and to the somewhat more distant end of the age. The sayings in Mk. 13 which refer to the Parousia are found in verses 5–8; 24–27, while verses 2:14–23 seem to have a more immediate implication. Mt. and Lk. contain apocalyptic details not found in Mk., but both (like Mk.) begin with the question about the future of the Temple. All three chapters contain predictions of the persecutions that will befall the faithful before the end of things.

[2] Mt. 24:43–25:13.

[3] Mt. 13:24–30; 36–43.

[4] Cf. Mt. 25:31ff., where the emphasis is on the good works that spring from faith.

sentence is postponed, judgment has already occurred in that men have judged themselves. The ministry of Jesus (and especially His death) is a *crisis* (Gk. *krisis* = judgment): the prince of this world has been judged,[1] the doom of the powers of evil pronounced, and by their alignment with one side or the other, men have already sealed their fate. We see then, that in New Testament teaching about Parousia and judgment, there is precisely the same tension between present and future realization that we noticed when discussing the Kingdom. This tension is true of all aspects of Christian eschatology, and indeed, of the redemptive process as a whole, and will call for further discussion at a later point.

The New Testament Letters. The letters of Paul contain many references to the Parousia, and it may be that the phrase *marana-tha* (Aramaic, *The Lord Comes!* or *Our Lord, Come!*)[2] was the watchword of the Church in his day. At all events, an early Parousia was certainly expected:

> Ye turned unto God from idols, to serve a living and true God, and to wait for his Son from heaven, whom he raised from the dead, even Jesus, which delivereth us from the wrath to come. (1 Thess. 1:9f.)

> To the end he may stablish your hearts unblameable in holiness before our God and Father, at the coming of our Lord Jesus with his saints. (1 Thess. 3:13)

These quotations from one of the earliest letters reveal Paul's mind at the beginning of his ministry; the Parousia is imminent, it will come upon his readers "like a thief in the night",[3] and they must not be caught unawares. In his second letter to Thessalonica, Paul mentions the Parousia as

[1] Jn. 16:11.
[2] 1 Cor. 16:22. According to *Didache*, 10:6, this phrase was used in the early Eucharistic liturgies.
[3] 1 Thess. 5:2; cf. 5:23.

bringing rest from persecution,[1] and later he speaks of the falling away of disciples and the slaying of the lawless one[2] that will precede the Coming—apocalyptic details which surely derive from Daniel 7:7; 8:23–25 etc. In the later epistles, Paul still speaks of a speedy Parousia;[3] the growth of the Church is evidence of the approach of Christ, and the Apostle looks for the end when Christ shall deliver up the Kingdom to God,[4] though such passages as 2 Corinthians 4:14, 16; 5:6f. suggest that he is no longer confident of living to see the events of which he writes.

Other New Testament writers speak of the nearness of the Parousia,[5] which will be heralded by rampaging wickedness, fiery trials, the appearance of antichrists etc. As in Old Testament apocalyptic, the message is that things must get worse before they get better! The writers of 2 Peter and Hebrews foresee the destruction of the wicked by fire,[6] while 1 John sees the world passing away—teaching reminiscent of Jesus's words in Mark 13:31, and indeed, of Psalm 102:26f. On the other hand, 2 Peter, alone of New Testament writers, prophesies the destruction of the earth by fire,[7] though this will not be the end of the material creation, for he looks for "new heavens and a new earth wherein dwelleth righteousness".[8] But this prediction of a catastrophic winding up of the present world-order is accompanied by the warning:

> But forget not this one thing, beloved, that one day is with the Lord as a thousand years, and a thousand years as one day. (2 Pet. 3:8)

[1] 2 Thess. 1:7.
[2] 2 Thess. 2:1–8.
[3] 1 Cor. 7:29; 10:11; Rom. 13:11; Phil. 3:20.
[4] 1 Cor. 15:24.
[5] Heb. 10:25; Jas. 5:7f.; 1 Pet. 4:5,7.
[6] Heb. 10:27,39; 2 Pet. 3:7.
[7] 2 Pet. 3:7,10,12.
[8] 2 Pet. 3:13.

It will not do to be too impatient; perhaps God appears slack, but that is only because He is long-suffering and wants all men to come to repentance. For this writer, as for the Evangelists, the Coming of the Lord is "as a thief in the night", and the need, therefore, is for a timely penitence.

The Book of Revelation (The Apocalypse). This book, as its name implies, is mainly concerned with visions of the end; what is only one facet of other New Testament writings, is here the main interest, and the mass of apocalyptic material can hardly be summarized in a paragraph. Like earlier books, Revelation stresses the nearness of the Parousia, and there are the admonitions to watch for its stealthy coming that we have met before. The teaching about the convulsions of Nature that will herald the Judgment can also be paralleled elsewhere, but there are other apocalyptic images which, though they may draw on material from the Old Testament and Jewish apocryphal books, are unique in the New Testament: (1) The appearance of the Dragon and his defeat in battle reminds us of Old Testament references to Yahweh's conquest of Leviathan and Rahab.[1] (2) The marriage of the Lamb and His bride,[2] which links the consummation of the Kingdom with the perfect union of the Church and her Lord. (3) The casting of Antichrist and the false prophets into the lake of fire, and the thousand-year imprisonment of Satan in the abyss,[3] which is reminiscent of the apocryphal Book of Enoch.[4] (4) The release of Satan and his stirring up of the nations (Gog and Magog; cf. Ezek. 38:3 before he is consigned to the lake.[5] (5) Christ and the saints and martyrs are to reign for a thousand years. This last is a new

---

[1] E.g. Ps. 74:13f.; Isa. 27:1; 51:9, etc.
[2] Rev. 19:6f. Cf. OT references to Yahweh's marriage of Israel.
[3] Rev. 19:11–20:3.
[4] Enoch 90:24f.
[5] Rev. 20:7–10.

element, and is the basis of *millenarian* or *chiliastic* teachings that have arisen in the Church from time to time, though it should be noted that Revelation does not assert that the thousand-year reign will be *on earth*, or that the existence of the martyrs and saints will be a *bodily* existence.

Throughout the New Testament, judgment is an important part of eschatology, but the details of what is sometimes called the Grand Assize or Last Judgment[1] vary. Sometimes it is God (i.e. the Father) who is to judge,[2] but more often it is Christ: "He hath given all judgment unto the Son."[3] Judgment is especially ascribed to Jesus in His rôle as Son of Man.[4] In some texts, disciples or saints are associated with Christ in judgment.[5] What is invariably clear is that final Judgment is linked with the coming of Christ (or Christ and the angels) in glory; that it is universal Judgment, and that men are judged according to their deeds.[6] It is a sobering thought that judgment must "begin at the house of God": there can never be any room for complacency, for we must all prepare to stand before the Judgment seat![7]

Resurrection and Future Life

Like most ancient peoples, the Israelites believed in some continued existence after death; archaeological evidence shows graves equipped with the personal belongings of the dead, and the story of the Witch of Endor[8] testifies to the belief that the spirits of great men, at least, could be recalled

[1] These are popular terms not found in the biblical text.

[2] Mt. 10:28; 18:35.

[3] Jn. 5-22; cf. 2 Cor. 5:10.

[4] Mt. 13:41; 25:31; Lk. 21:36.

[5] Mt. 19:28; 1 Cor. 6:2f.

[6] Mt. 25:14–30, 31–46; Rom. 2:5f.; 2 Cor. 5:10.

[7] 1 Pet. 4:17.

[8] 1 Sam. 28:3–25.

(soon) after death, though necromancy was certainly a forbidden art, no doubt practised covertly.[1] But the existence of the departed in the underworld, *Sheol* (sometimes called "the Pit") was a shadowy existence in which all men were reduced to weakness and futility:

> For of the wise man, even as of the fool, there is no remembrance for ever . . . and how doth the wise man die even as the fool! (Eccles. 2:16)

> Art thou also become weak as we? art thou become like unto us? Thy pomp is brought down to Sheol . . . (Is. 14:10f.)[2]

Death is the great leveller! Existence in Sheol can hardly be called future *life*,[3] and of course it has nothing whatever to do with resurrection; indeed there is no firm Old Testament evidence of belief in resurrection, except in two[4] very late passages:

> Thy dead shall live; my dead bodies shall arise. Awake and sing, ye that dwell in the dust: for thy dew is as the dew of herbs, and the earth shall cast forth the dead. (Is. 26:19)

> And many of them that sleep in the dust of the earth shall awake, some to everlasting life, and some to shame and everlasting contempt. (Dan. 12:2)

Both passages refer to judgment, and it was probably the despair of ever obtaining justice in this life that led men to look for a resurrection in which all would receive their deserts. Very late in Judaism, Greek notions of the im-

---

[1] Deut. 18:9–11; Isa. 8:19.

[2] Part of a taunting song for the King of Babylon.

[3] It has been said that Sheol represented the persistence of death rather than the persistence of life!

[4] Despite Handel's *Messiah*, Job 19:25f., which is very uncertain in the Hebrew, probably does not refer to resurrection—so NEB and most modern scholars. Some passages in Psalms have been claimed as evidence for the future life (Ps. 16:10f.; 17:15; 49:15; 73:26; 139:7–12), but their meaning is very unclear.

mortality of the soul appear in Jewish literature,[1] and in the apocalyptic period between the Testaments, we see a great development of the idea of retribution beyond this life, though in some passages resurrection is only for those who have not been rewarded or punished during life, and not necessarily for all.[2]

In Jesus's lifetime, Jewish opinion was still very divided on the subject. The Pharisees and most ordinary folk believed in life after death, while the priestly[3] sect of the Sadducees (who accepted as doctrine only what could be proved from the Pentateuch), just as strongly denied it. Where the common people stood is probably represented by Martha's affirmation, "I know that he shall rise again in the resurrection at the last day".[4] But that belief goes beyond anything explicitly taught in the canonical Jewish scriptures, and rests upon a rabbinic interpretation which was really a reading of Old Testament texts in the light of a philosophical doctrine of immortality,[5] and an apocalyptic expectation of a general righting of wrongs on the Day of the Lord.

The dreary, half-existence of Sheol which, in earlier Judaism was the indifferent fate of good and bad, great and small, had to be modified to accommodate the ideas of reward and punishment meted out after death. For the wicked there is hell—*Gehenna*,[6] the place of fiery torment, and for the

---

[1] Wisd. 5:15; 8:19f.; Enoch 23:5.

[2] So Enoch 22:9-13.

[3] All priests were Sadducees, but not all Sadducees were priests. Some were wealthy landowners, and probably some were scribes.

[4] Jn. 11:24.

[5] Through the Dispersion, Jews came into contact with Greek ideas and (especially in Alexandria) attempt was made to reinterpret OT religion in their light. The most notable writers of this School were Aristobulus (second century B.C.), Pseudo-Aristeas (100 B.C.) and Philo (b. about 20 B.C.).

[6] From *Ge-Hinnom*, a valley near Jerusalem, once the scene of child sacrifice, and later a smoking garbage dump.

righteous, *Paradise*[1] or *Abraham's Bosom*.[2] Most likely, both the abode of the blessed and Gehenna were thought of as divisions of Sheol in which good and bad experienced a preparatory reward or punishment[3] before the final Judgment, though this is uncertain.

What does seem clear, is that Judaism never envisaged a disembodied existence: for the Jew (who saw man as an animated body rather than an embodied spirit), such an idea was unthinkable, as we shall see when we consider St. Paul's teaching about the Resurrection. Probably, too, when Jews thought of resurrection, they thought of it as a rising to life *on earth*—perhaps even as a mere restoration of life as it had been before death,[4] though again we cannot be sure. In first-century Judaism there was, as we have seen, considerable diversity of opinion. Happily, the infant Church did not base its hope of resurrection and the future life upon questionable rabbinic teaching, or on its own reading of the more hopeful Old Testament texts, but upon the certain fact of the Resurrection of Jesus Christ.

The Teaching of Jesus. Jesus said that the Sadducees were wrong in denying resurrection; they erred, *"not knowing the Scriptures nor the power of God"*. (Matthew 22:29) Resurrection must be a fact, because a living God can hardly be the God of the dead, and therefore *all live unto Him*. (Luke 20:38) The Lucan version of the disputation is particularly interesting in its additions to the Markan narrative. Jesus speaks of a conditional resurrection:

[1] From the word for a Persian nobleman's garden: to the Jew, it no doubt recalled Eden.

[2] I.e. the immediate presence of "the Friend of God".

[3] Perhaps *one* source of RC ideas of Purgatory, but the latter, though it involves painful purification, does not involve destruction.

[4] *Apoc. Baruch*, 49–51; 2 Macc. 14:46!

> They that are accounted worthy to attain to that world, and the resurrection from the dead neither marry nor are given in marriage: For neither can they die any more: for they are equal unto the angels; and are sons of God, being sons of the resurrection. (Lk. 20:35f.)

It is, apparently, only the righteous who rise, but when they do, it is to *eternal* life. This resurrection of the righteous to be rewarded occurs in another passage peculiar to Luke: "For thou shalt be recompensed in the resurrection of the just." (Lk. 14:14) The Fourth Gospel, on the other hand, says:

> The hour cometh and now is, when the dead shall hear the voice of the Son of God; and they that hear shall live ... for the hour cometh, in which all who are in the tombs shall hear his voice, And shall come forth; they that have done good, unto the resurrection of life; and they that have done ill, unto the resurrection of judgment. (Jn. 5:25, 28f.)

Here it is not certain whether all, or only some hear the voice and rise, but the apparent contradiction can be removed by referring verse 25 to the *spiritually dead*, as against the physically dead of verses 28 and 29. In that case, the latter verses speak of a general resurrection, and one that will come soon. An earlier verse[1] affirms that, for the believer in Christ, eternal life is a present possession—he "cometh not into judgment, but hath passed out of death into life". One further passage must be cited—the word of Jesus to the dying thief. Here there is no explicit mention of resurrection, but the promise is implicit in the assurance, "Today shalt thou be with me in Paradise".[2]

The Resurrection of Jesus. The earliest account of the Easter Event is that in 1 Corinthians 15:4ff., which summarizes the Resurrection appearances recorded in the Gospels, with the addition of an appearance to James,[3] and one to

[1] Jn. 5:24.   [2] Lk. 23:43.   [3] The brother of Jesus.

five hundred brethren together. Paul speaks of the Resurrection as taking place *according to the Scriptures*, but cites no specific Old Testament text. The Gospel accounts[1] record the visit of the women to the garden, where they find the tomb empty. Luke and John report the visit of Peter (or Peter and John) to the tomb to verify the women's story, and both include other Resurrection appearances in Judaea and Galilee.

These accounts make it clear that Jesus appeared only to His followers, and that in His appearances He was possessed of some qualities that belong to the natural body—His frame was tangible, and He could eat;[2] on the other hand, He was capable of passing through closed doors and of appearing and disappearing at will,[3] which are powers not associated with the body as we know it.

The Resurrection of Christians. The assurance of resurrection is based not on religious or philosophical grounds, but on the Resurrection of Jesus and His promises to the Disciples,[4] and again, the resurrection of believers is spoken of both as a future event, and as already attained:

> For if we have become united with him by the likeness of his death, we shall be also by the likeness of his resurrection.[5] (Rom. 6:5)

> If then ye were raised together with Christ, seek the things that are above, where Christ is, seated on the right hand of God. (Col. 3:1)[6]

But it is not believers only who will be raised, for "there shall be a resurrection both of the just and unjust".[7] What

[1] Mk. 16:1–8 (see NEB footnote); Mt. 28; Lk. 24; Jn. 20–21.
[2] Mt. 28:9f.; Lk. 24:39ff.; Jn. 20:27.
[3] Lk. 24:15,31; Jn. 20:19,26.
[4] Jn. 6:39f.; 14:1ff.; Rom. 14:8f., etc.
[5] Cf. also Rom. 8:11; Phil. 3:11.
[6] Cf. also Eph. 2:6.
[7] Acts 24:15.

the resurrection life will be like, the New Testament does not reveal. Paul infers, from the variety of bodies in nature, that we shall hereafter have new and different bodies appropriate to the new life; as a Jew, he could not contemplate an incorporeal existence.[1] But precisely what that "spiritual body" will be like, we cannot know. The last word must be the reverent agnosticism of the writer of 1 John:

> Now we are children of God, and it is not yet made manifest what we shall be. We know that, if he shall be manifested, we shall be like him ... (1 Jn. 3:2)

[1] 1 Cor. 15:44; 2 Cor. 5:1-4.

II

HISTORICAL DEVELOPMENT AND CONSTRUCTIVE STATEMENT

1. Historical Development

Christians have not always been content to remain in ignorance, and eschatology has a strange fascination for some religious minds. Throughout the Christian era, individuals and sects have ransacked the apocalyptic passages of Ezekiel, Daniel and Revelation and with great ingenuity have deduced from them the time and circumstances of the end of this world-order. Every political crisis or natural disaster has been the occasion for eccentrics to don the prophetic mantle and foretell the imminent cataclysm.[1]

But this has always been a minority activity; the Church has eschewed attempts to be precise about the timing of the Parousia or the order of events in the last days, and has never committed herself to detailed statements. While mediums have arisen from very early times, orthodoxy has condemned spiritualistic attempts to make contact with "the next world"

---

[1] In particular, there has been great speculation about "the number of the beast" (Rev. 13:18) which has been made to refer to the Kaiser, Hitler and others. The end of the world has been predicted for the years 1000, 1914, 1944 etc. and the appearance of a comet has often been held to pressage the end.

as firmly as the Old Testament condemned necromancy.

For the churchman, eschatological doctrine is expressed in quite general statements about the Second Coming, the Last Judgment, the Resurrection of the Dead and the Life Everlasting. The Creeds do not go beyond Scripture.

Kingdom of God. Two main problems have recurred: first, the relationship of Church and Kingdom which was discussed earlier, and second, whether the Kingdom is to be regarded as present or future. As we have seen, there is a tension in Scripture between the Kingdom announced by Jesus as a present reality calling for immediate response—the *realized eschatology* view, and as something that will appear suddenly and unexpectedly in the last times—*futurist eschatology.*

At the beginning of the present century, Albert Schweitzer,[1] reacting against nineteenth-century tendencies to discount the eschatological passages in the Gospels as due to the beliefs of the disciples, maintained, to the contrary, that eschatology was essential to the understanding of a Jesus who saw Himself as an apocalyptic figure, and who deliberately took upon Himself the woes of suffering and death associated with the last times. According to Schweitzer, Jesus certainly looked for the approaching end.

At the other pole, C. H. Dodd[2] maintained that the Kingdom, in all its essentials, came in with Jesus, whose life, ministry, death and Resurrection were themselves the fulfilment of the ancient prophecies and apocalyptic hopes. On this view, Jesus was not much interested in the future, and the apocalyptic passages in the New Testament have to be attributed to the Early Church rather than to Him.

A middle view is represented by R. H. Fuller:[3] Jesus saw

---

[1] *The Quest of the Historical Jesus* (ET 1910).

[2] *The Apostolic Preaching and its Development* (1936). R. Otto, J. Jeremias and O. Cullmann are other prominent members of the *realized eschatology* School.

[3] *The Mission and Achievement of Jesus* (1954).

His ministry as *inaugurating* the Kingdom, but looked to its fulfilment through His sufferings, death and Resurrection. Each of these views can claim support from some of the sayings of Jesus, and all are valuable insights, but none can be expected to resolve the paradox that runs not only through the Gospels, but through all the New Testament writings.

The Parousia. In the Patristic period, the generally accepted chronology was six ages[1] of one thousand years each; Christ had come at the beginning of the sixth age, and would come again at its end.[2] Another common view was that the six thousand years would be followed by the first resurrection of the righteous, who would then enjoy the millennium, a thousand-year reign of Christ. The idea of an earthly reign of Christ was beloved of heretical sects like the Ebionites[3] and Montanists.[4] Augustine,[5] however, believed the thousand years of Revelation 20:4f. to be the duration of the Church on earth, and this became accepted doctrine. Gradually, millenarian views largely died out in the Church, though they were revived from time to time when some great catastrophe—the fall of Rome, an earthquake or plague—led to widespread forebodings. After the Reformation, millenarian views were held by many Anabaptists, and in modern times they are characteristic of the American sects, Seventh Day Adventists, Second Adventists and Jehovah's Witnesses.

Resurrection and Future Life. In contrast with the Parousia, which must affect all men together, resurrection and future

[1] Corresponding to the six days of Creation.

[2] Hippolytus, *de Christo et Antichristo*, expected the end in 250 years, Lactantius in 200. Many early Christians thought the consummation would come in A.D. 1000.

[3] A second-century Judaizing sect who rejected Paulinism and accepted only Matthew's Gospel.

[4] They expected the New Jerusalem to come down from heaven to a lonely village in Asia Minor.

[5] *City of God*, XXI, 6f.

life are essentially personal and individual, and the questions that have been asked by Christians have therefore been more particular. Does each believer rise immediately at death, or must all wait for a general resurrection? What is the fate of the Old Testament saints and sages who died before Christ "brought life and incorruption to light through the Gospel"? Do the wicked suffer eternal punishment, or are their souls extinguished?

The first of these questions is unreal in the light of a true understanding of *eternity*, and to that we shall return in the next section. The second question also really hinges on the same point, and the mind of ordinary Christians can perhaps be judged by the works of early artists, who depicted Old Testament figures in the crowd on Calvary and therefore, by implication, included them in the benefits of the Passion.

The fate of the wicked, luridly portrayed by artists and preachers throughout many centuries, is not so easily dealt with.

Augustine,[1] Aquinas and Calvin saw the wicked as condemned eternally, but in ancient and modern times, some churchmen have rebelled against a teaching that represents divine justice as harsher than man's, and against the conclusion that God's redemptive purpose is apparently eternally frustrated if some men are to be finally lost. The alternative is some form of *universalism*, regarding hell as a purgative experience from which men emerge when their sins have been expiated. This view was held by Clement of Alexandria, Gregory of Nyssa, and Origen,[2] but was condemned by the Council of Constantinople in A.D. 543. After the Reformation, similar views were held by Anabaptists and Moravians, and in modern times are often maintained by Liberal Protestants. Some theologians have claimed Christ's descent into hell (I Pet. 3:19; 4:6)—what is called the "harrowing of

[1] Esp. *City of God.*
[2] Origen held that the Devil himself would finally be saved.

hell"—as evidence that, even in the infernal regions, men (and perhaps fallen angels) may have a further chance of salvation, and indeed, there is usually some element of further chance in any universalist theory. The Petrine text is reflected in Langland, *Piers Plowman*:

> My righteousness and right shall rule all Hell, and give mercy to mankind before me in Heaven. I were an unkind king, save I my kind help—

but has never greatly attracted most scholars—perhaps because it lacks other scriptural support.[1]

On any further-chance view, hell becomes a sort of Purgatory, and the question naturally arises whether we on earth can influence the state and prospects of the wicked undergoing punishment.

In the Middle Ages, the Church sold *indulgences* guaranteeing remission of the penalties of the living on earth, the dead in Purgatory, or both—a system based on current satisfactionist theories of the Atonement and on the Church's right, through the "power of the keys"[2] to draw on the fund of Grace accumulated for her by Christ and the saints. It was the scandals of the sale of indulgences that led Luther to formulate the famous *Ninety-five Theses* which sparked-off the Protestant Reformation. Since then, Roman Catholics have largely abandoned this gross distortion of the doctrine of Grace, though they, and many modern Protestants, continue to pray for the souls of the departed[3]—a very different matter from *paying* for them!

The modern period, with its more scientific cosmology, has seen the abandonment of earlier ideas of a hell below the earth and a heaven (or heavens) above. Spatial metaphors of

[1] Perhaps it has some support in Jn. 5:19–29, and possibly also in Mt. 5:26; 12:32.

[2] Mt. 16:19.

[3] A very ancient practice; cf. 2 Macc. 12:39ff., possibly 2 Tim. 1:18.

this kind are now seen to be unsatisfactory, and heaven and hell are increasingly regarded as *states*, not places; admission to or exclusion from the Presence of God being an altogether more spiritual understanding of the life to come.

The same process of spiritualization has transformed our understanding of the nature of resurrection. While some New Testament passages speak of the resurrection body as identical with the body before death,[1] the resurrection appearances of Jesus, and the general New Testament view of the risen life of men, make it clear that the risen body is to be a glorified body, and the future life a life free of sensual desires.[2] From this, it follows that references to feasting and harp-playing etc. by the blessed, and the fiery torments of the wicked, are alike symbolic.

While this was understood by Christians from early times, much of what was written indicates that the future life was often unconsciously thought of in physical and material terms; real fire is hardly an appropriate torment for *souls*, but that was the way that punishment was generally pictured. Similarly, the article in the Apostles' Creed, "I believe in the resurrection of the body", was long understood in a literal sense that made Christians unwilling to cremate their dead.[3] Nowadays, Christians think rather of the continuation of recognizable *personality* after death, and the old horror of destroying corpses by fire, or using them for medical purposes, is no longer felt.

2. Constructive Statement

For a generation, realized eschatology has largely held the field, and the Parousia has been regarded as already fulfilled

[1] Mt. 5:29f.; 10:28; Rom. 8:11,23; 1 Cor. 15:53.
[2] Mk. 12:25, etc.
[3] Cremation had been common in pre-Christian times, though not among the Jews.

in the events of the Gospels. Now, however, the theological pendulum is swinging back, and the current Theology of Hope School[1] is inclined to look for a future return of Christ and a cataclysmic end of the world-order, though at a date that cannot be predicted. Eschatology is again being taken seriously by reputable theologians, and there is now a greater willingness to accept that the bulk of the New Testament, and certainly the earliest stratum, regarded the coming again in glory as a distinctly future event though, as it turned out, an event that was to be longer delayed than the first Christians expected.

An eventual end to the present world-order was never in serious doubt; creation is finite, and must have an end as it had a beginning. What was (and is) in doubt was the nature of the end. Will the universe gradually run down, or will it end dramatically by the direct intervention of the Creator, once it has ceased to have any purpose? On the whole, a sudden end to the world seems more in character with the God of Christian revelation than a slow fizzling out of what is, after all, the stage on which the drama of salvation has been set.

There is no reason for ruling out a second Coming of Christ, and certainly no reason for doubting a Final Judgment. What Scripture records is a succession of mighty acts of God— the Creation, the Exodus, the Incarnation, the Crucifixion and Resurrection—all parts of the plan of Redemption; and the nature of God seems to require that His plan shall ultimately be accomplished. Some sort of eschatology is essential if we are to speak of salvation *history*, with a moral goal to be reached, and not simply of events going endlessly

[1] In this School are included the German Protestants, J. Moltmann (*Theology of Hope*, ET 1967), W. Pannenberg (*Jesus, God and Man*, 1968), the German Roman Catholic, J. Metz (*Theology of the World*, 1969), along with C. E. Braaten in the U.S.A., R. Alves in Brazil, and others.

on or ceaselessly round and round: indeed, the nature of man as a responsible moral agent appears to require some ultimate reckoning. We need not, of course, take the apocalyptic imagery associated with the last times to be other than symbolic of the power of God suddenly and dramatically revealed, and we must not meddle with what is not our business by trying to say when the end will be.

Mention of final judgment raises the question of eternal reward and punishment, and the question of what happens to the dead in the interval before the end. While the nature of time and eternity is too complex for finite minds, an attempt must be made to remove misconceptions that needlessly trouble some Christians.

Time and Eternity.[1] The Bible takes history seriously; time and space are not illusory, but they are not the only realities either. When the Bible says that a thousand years and one day are alike to God,[2] it is stating the plain fact that Time does not mean to God what it means to us. A moment's reflection shows that Time is relative—relative to our place on this particular planet. Conceivably, we might have been born on a planet in which a day is longer than a year![3] Since God created the universe of space-time, clearly He is not bound by it any more than a dramatist is bound by the time and location of his play. When we speak of the Patriarchs living *before* Christ, or the dead waiting *until* the resurrection of the just, we are looking at things from the human point of view; for God there is no before, or after, or until. The Schoolmen said that God saw past, present and future as one

---

[1] For valuable discussions of this subject see R. Niebuhr, *The Nature and Destiny of Man* (1941), O. Cullmann, *Christ and Time* (1951), and J. Marsh, *The Fullness of Time* (1952). Also P. Tillich, *Systematic Theology III*, whose distinction between *chronos* (clock time) and *Kairos* (season, opportunity) has been immensely influential.

[2] Ps. 90:4; 2 Pet. 3:8.

[3] E.g. the planet, Venus.

moment of Time—and that, probably, is as far as our finite notions can go.

But we must be careful: it is not just that we live in Time and *then* pass into eternity (though from our point of view, we do), but that Time is *within* eternity as a point may be within a circle. What happens to the world, from the divine view-point, is presumably, *time-less*, and all the events of salvation history are both in Time, and transcendent of Time. The Cross, for instance, had its own time and place, but it is also a Cross *towering o'er the wrecks of time*—a decisive, timeless expression of God's love, and every bit as capable of redeeming Noah and the modern Christian, as of saving the people of first-century Palestine. Once we get rid of the idea that space-time limits God, there is also less difficulty about *eternal punishment*, which is quite indefensible and morally repugnant if thought of as inflicted for an infinity of years. Similarly, no question need arise about the state of the dead awaiting judgment. The dead are not *awaiting* anything, for they have already passed from the sphere of Time, and when the New Testament speaks of an immediate resurrection at death and of a general resurrection in the last times, there is no real contradiction.

Resurrection and Future Life. In some recent theology,[1] there has been a tendency to think of the Resurrection of Jesus as something that happened to (or in) the Disciples, rather than as an objective fact of history, and to regard the evidence of the empty tomb as a mistaken addition to the Gospel text, made by Jesus's simple but well-meaning followers. The opposite tendency is now asserting itself, and scholars are more ready to accept the Gospel narrative and to think of the

[1] E.g. R. Bultmann and the Demythologising School, a Movement which interpreted the NT in *existential* rather than *historial* terms. See Bultmann's *Jesus Christ and Mythology* (ET 1960), J. Macquarrie, *An Existentialist Theology* (1955), and L. Malevez (a Jesuit), *The Christian Message and Myth* (1958).

Resurrection as a real event in Time. This is a welcome change, for there is no sound reason for doubting the word of Gospel writers not otherwise known to be untruthful, and certainly none for denying the *possibility* of the Resurrection. What happened to the body of Jesus at the Resurrection (or at the Ascension) is a mystery, and how it differed from the body He had before death is not altogether clear, but in the light of modern scientific understanding of matter as *energy*, we have no right to rule out the possibility of a change from one form to another. The resurrection body of Jesus needed to be displayed in a way that ours will not be, and it may be that God used unusual means to effect a unique event.

It is clear that Jesus's resurrection body was somehow different. John 20:14 and Luke 24:13–30 show that His friends did not immediately recognize Him even when they were thinking or talking about Him, but that they did know Him at once when, by a characteristic word or action, His personality showed through.[1] Evidently His body was changed in appearance, and was free from some, at least, of the ordinary limitations of Time and space, but it *was* the vehicle of recognizable personality. He was the same Jesus they had always known.

Christian belief in the future life rests upon the raising of Jesus from the dead, and we may expect that our resurrection bodies will be different just as His was. Paul's words about the *spiritual body*, and the credal phrase, *the resurrection of the body* are alike intended to safeguard the *reality* of life beyond death. This risen life is no imaginary or ghostly thing; our personalities or *egos*—what we mean when we say *I* or *me*— will live on in whatever form is appropriate to a mode of existence that, in our earthly life, we can hardly imagine. As life in the world is personally continuous with previous life in the womb, though possessed of wider freedom and new

[1] Jn. 20:16; Lk. 24:30f.

powers of sight and movement etc., we may expect the life to come to be a further liberation and enrichment.

But we can no more expect to know what that wider life will be like, than could an unborn child (if capable of rational thought) picture life outside his mother's body! What we do know is that the believer enters, here and now, into a quality of life (*zōē aionios = eternal life*) that will survive death, with the ego not only unimpaired but enlarged, albeit after death, in a new form, suited to the transition from the here into the everywhere. What then happens to the physical body, is a matter of indifference.

Conditional Immortality and Universalism. But what happens to those who are not in a faithful relationship with Christ? As we have seen, the Bible does not support the unconditional immortality of the soul: "Dust thou art, and unto dust shalt thou return." (Gen. 3:19) Granted human free will, some may spurn the appeal of divine love and thereby lose the eternal life with God that is the reward of the faithful, but we remember that God wills the salvation of all, and therefore the ultimate redemption of *mankind* cannot be ruled out. The mercy that presides over all God's works may yet find a way to avoid the loss of those who, in life, appear unresponsive to the overtures of love. Despite Augustine and Calvin, universalism is certainly attractive; while God's judgment on sin is written large on every page of scripture, that judgment is conditioned by His Fatherhood. When all is said and done, God's eternal nature is *Love*, not judgment!

The end of time will come, but we must not try to probe beyond what Scripture tells us about it. We are not required to understand the ultimate purposes of God, but to respond individually to the immediate offer of salvation, and then to work collectively in the Church for the evangelization of the world. The Exalted One inhabits eternity, but He dwells also with the contrite and humble to revive their spirits,[1] and

[1] Isa. 57:15.

120

eschatology is useful as a warning to us to repent, that we may be ready to receive Him. The nail was hit squarely on the head by one of the old teachers of Israel:

> Rabbi Eliezer said, "Repent one day before your death." His disciples asked him, "Does, then, anybody know on which day he will die?" He replied to them, "How much more reason is there for him to repent to-day, lest he be dead tomorrow?"[1]

And repentance is not a matter of forms and ceremonies only. As the Jewish congregations were admonished on fast days:

> Brethren, it is not said of the men of Nineveh, "And God saw their sackcloth and their fasting", but, "God saw that they turned from their evil way".[2]

It is repentance and faith, and the works that flow from them that matter, and in the end, the doctrines that we have discussed are important and valuable only insofar as they lead to a saving relationship with the God, who at creation gave men life, and in Christ gives them life eternal. Theology, like the Gospel on which it rests, is written: *That ye may believe that Jesus is the Christ, the Son of God; and that believing, ye may have life in his name.* (Jn. 20:31.)

---

[1] Shab. 153a, quoted A. Cohen, *Everyman's Talmud*, 110.
[2] Taan II.1 (Cohen, *op. cit.*, p. 103).

List of Words

ANABAPTISTS, literally "re-baptisers". The name for several extremist sects that arose (especially in Germany and Switzerland) out of the Reformation. Anabaptists insisted on adult baptism and rejected the infant rite. Usually, they were pacifist, and refused to take part in civil affairs. Their religion was mystical, and they strove to establish a Church that was entirely without spot and blemish. The sect was much persecuted both for its theological and its political views.

ANTHROPOMORPHISM, the representation of God as having the thoughts, feelings and even the form of man. Thus to speak of "God's mighty arm" is an anthropomorphism.

APOCALYPSE, the Greek title of the last book in the NT, the most important Christian example of apocalyptic literature. The word is also used of any book or passage written in the apocalyptic style.

APOCALYPTIC, a form of Jewish literature in which the future (or the last things) is revealed, often in the form of dreams and visions. The language of apocalyptic is highly-coloured, and there is great use of symbolism. Whereas, in Hebrew prophecy, inspired individuals directly confronted their generation with a divine message relevant to the immediate situation, apocalyptists generally wrote under an assumed name (usually that of some great figure of the past), and concerned themselves only with far-off events. In later Judaism, apocalyptic tended to replace prophecy, but there is no firm dividing line, and elements of the former are found in the latter. The later the date of a prophetic writing, the more likely it is to contain apocalyptic material. The *Dead Sea Scrolls* include apocalyptic works (e.g. *The War of the Sons of Light against the Sons of Darkness*), which is valuable independent evidence of the currency of this type of literature in the Jewish world at the beginning of our era. (R. H. Charles (ed.), *The Apocrypha and Pseudepigrapha of the Old Testament*, two vols. (1913); H. H. Rowley, *The Relevance of Apocalyptic*, 2nd edition (1947); C. C. Torrey, *The Apocryphal Literature*, 1945; M. Burrows, *More Light on the Dead Sea Scrolls*, 1958.)

APOCRYPHA, a collection of Jewish writings included in the Septuagint and regarded as sacred by Greek-speaking, but not by Hebrew-speaking Jews in the time of Jesus. Accepted by Christians in the first four centuries, they were relegated to an inferior category by Jerome in his Latin Vulgate translation. Since the Reformation, some churches have regarded the Apocrypha as useful in morals, but not for doctrine, and in certain communions, the books are omitted altogether from public reading. The Council of Trent allowed the collection full canonicity.

CHARISMATIC, having, or being dependent upon grace.
CHILIASM, *see* MILLENARIANISM.
CONCUPISCENCE, sexual appetite.

DEMYTHOLOGISING, the attempt to translate the "myth" of the NT into the terms of human existence. It should be said that "myth" is here used not in its popular sense, but for the whole theology and philosophy of the NT. Originated by Rudolph Bultmann, the Movement represents a systematic interpretation of the NT in the thought-forms of existentialist philosophy. (R. Bultmann, *New Testament and Mythology*, 1941: *Theology of the New Testament*, two vols., ET 1952, 1955.)

ESCHATOLOGY, the doctrine of the last things.

EXISTENTIALISM, a type of philosophy maintaining that the values of goodness, truth, beauty etc. are not external objective realities, but are to be created by man out of his own experience of intense living. The term is a loose one used of many different but related views, most of which owe something at least to the writings of the nineteenth-century religious thinker, Søren Kierkegäard. Leading Existentialists include Martin Heidegger, Karl Jaspers, Gabriel Marcel, Martin Buber, Jean-Paul Sartre, Paul Tillich. (H. J. Blackham, *Six Existentialist Thinkers*, 1952; D. E. Roberts, *Existentialism and Religious Belief*, 1957.)

GLOSSOLALIA, "the gift of tongues", utterances made (in no known language) under the stress of intense religious emotion. The phenomenon was apparently common in the Early Church, and still occurs especially in Pentecostalist sects. Where glossolalia is practised, the presence of some inspired person to interpret the utterance is required.

GOG AND MAGOG. In Ezek. 38–39, Gog is a prince, and Magog the land that he rules. In later apocalyptic writings, they usually stand for the world hostile to the people of God, i.e. the nations in a bad sense. Gog and Magog have that meaning (the nations subject to Satan) in Rev. 20:8, their only NT occurrence.

HELLENISTIC, Greek, especially Greek culture and thought-forms in the ancient world.

IMMACULATE CONCEPTION, the dogma, defined by Pope Pius IX in 1854, that Mary, the mother of Jesus, was conceived free from every stain of original guilt. It does not mean that she lacked either human parent, but that she received at conception the grace that Christians normally receive at baptism. The doctrine (which lacks any biblical foundation) is binding upon Roman Catholics but is generally rejected by Orthodox and Protestant Christians.

IMMANENCE, the doctrine that God's presence pervades the whole universe. If pressed too far, the doctrine becomes PANTHEISM—the identification of God with the universe.

IMMUTABILITY, the doctrine of God's changelessness. Theologians often held not only that God was changeless, but that He was incapable of change.

INFRALAPSARIANISM (or SUBLAPSARIANISM), the commoner Calvinist view that God, in making the eternal decrees of predestination to election and damnation, was contemplating man as we know him, created and Fallen.

LOGICAL POSITIVISM. POSITIVISM is a type of philosophy that rejects metaphysics, theology and all knowledge gained "negatively" by conjecture, and allows only what can be known "positively" by experience and observation. The founder of modern Positivism was Auguste Comte (1798–1857). LOGICAL POSITIVISM is a more radical branch of Positivism holding that a statement has meaning only if it can be verified or falsified by experience. On this view metaphysical and theological statements are dismissed as meaningless and are therefore incapable of being discussed. The weakness of the system is, of course, that Logical Positivist theory cannot be tested by experience either.

LOGOS (Gk. = word, reason), a term used in the prologue to the Fourth Gospel as a designation of the Eternal Word of God through whom creation came to be, and who became incarnate in Jesus. The roots of Logos doctrine are in the OT and Apocrypha, where the creative word of God (and the wisdom of God) appear prominently, but it may also owe something to the writings of the Jewish philosopher, Philo of Alexandria (*d.* about A.D. 40), who used logos, a current Greek philosophical concept, in his attempt to interpret Hebrew religion in terms of Greek thought. Greek philosophers who used the Logos concept include Heraclitus, Plato and the Stoics.

MACEDONIANS, also called PNEUMATOMACHI— "fighters against the spirit". Said to be the followers of Macedonius, they were condemned at the Council of Ephesus, A.D. 381. They denied the full divinity of the Holy Spirit in the same way that Arians denied the full divinity of the Son.

MILLENARIANISM, MILLENNIANISM, the teaching that the return of Christ will be preceded by a thousand-year reign of the saints. The idea is derived from Jewish apocalyptic *via* Rev. 20:1–7. It was held by some heretical sects in the Early Church, was later revived by Anabaptists, and is now found among modern Adventists.

MORTAL SINS, sins that lead to eternal damnation if the sinner dies unrepentant, though they can be removed by the sacramental grace of the Church. Contrasted with VENIAL SINS which are either less serious or, if mortal in gravity, were committed in ignorance or in the heat of the moment. Venial sins can be expiated by penance. Protestants reject this Catholic distinction and regard *all* sin as requiring penitence, not penance, for its removal.

NECROMANCY, the art of recalling and consulting the dead with a view to obtaining guidance about the future. The modern derivative is spiritualism.

OMNIPOTENCE, the doctrine that there is no limit to the power of God.

OMNISCIENCE, the parallel doctrine that there is no limit to God's knowledge.

ONTOLOGY, the science of being, that branch of metaphysics which deals with the nature or essence of things. The ONTOLOGICAL ARGUMENT for the existence of God, devised by St. Anselm (1033–1109) says that God, defined as a Being than which no greater can be conceived, must exist because a being that existed in thought only would not be as great as one existing in both thought and fact; therefore God must necessarily exist. Descartes revived the argument in the form that the idea of God, who is perfect and infinite, cannot be formed in man by any finite object and must therefore be caused by God himself. Spinoza also used the argument, but it was firmly rejected by Kant and since his day has not generally been advanced in either of the above forms. Nevertheless, this argument is suggestive and, taken with others, still has some force.

PARACLETE (Gk. = advocate, intercessor, comforter), a designation of the Holy Spirit used only in the Fourth Gospel.
PAROUSIA, the Greek word for the return of Christ or "second coming". The other (Latin) name for the same event is second (or properly, "last") advent.
PATRISTIC, pertaining to the Fathers, Christian writers of the first few centuries. Writers of the period immediately following the NT are known as the APOSTOLIC FATHERS.
PENTATEUCH, the first five books of the OT attributed to Moses and referred to as "the Law". Sadducees accepted only the Pentateuch as authoritative for doctrine, but Pharisees recognised also the PROPHETS—both the historical books (Jos., Jud., Sam. etc.) which were known as the *former prophets*, and Isaiah to Malachi, called the *latter prophets*.

REATUS, a term used especially by seventeenth-century Protestant theologians, who distinguished between *reatus culpae*—"guilt" and *reatus poenae*—"liability to punishment".

SEPTUAGINT (LXX), the most important Greek translation of the OT and Apocrypha, and the only one that is certainly pre-Christian. So called because of the tradition that

127

seventy-two elders (six from each of the twelve tribes of Israel) completed the translation in seventy-two days.

SOCINIANS, the followers of Faustus Socinus of Siena (1539–1604). Influenced by Italian humanism, Socinus developed a "liberal" form of Christianity which rejected the formulations of the great Church Councils, especially those dealing with the Person of Christ. Socinian ideas affected some seventeenth and eighteenth-century English churchmen, and were reflected in the liberalism and latitudinarianism of that period.

SUPRALAPSARIANISM, the minority Calvinist view that the eternal divine decrees were made for man not yet created and only *liable* to fall. (*See* INFRALAPSARIANISM.)

THEOPHANY, the appearance of God to man.

THOMISM (adj. THOMIST), the theology and philosophy of St. Thomas Aquinas.

TRIDENTINE, pertaining to the Council of Trent.

TRIUNE NAME, the name of God as Father, Son and Holy Spirit. Triune means "three in one".

VITIUM, immorality, depravity, vice.